SIBLING TRANSFERENCE IN THERAPY

THE IMPACT OF SIBLING TRANSFERENCE AND
COUNTERTRANSFERENCE IN ADULT PSYCHOTHERAPY

By

MARCY STITES

In loving memory to my niece, Robin Stites, and to Sue Saperstein for all her help and support, making this work possible

Preface

The topic of sibling transference has been neglected in both theory and training. This book looks at results of a study conducted in 1997 that examined sibling transference and countertransference in adult psychotherapy. Sixteen psychotherapists practicing from a psychoanalytic perspective were interviewed using a structured questionnaire. Respondents were asked questions about the following topic areas: How does sibling transference manifest in treatment; which factors in particular seem to elicit or contribute to the development of sibling transference; what are the analytic dynamics of sibling transference; is the subject of sibling transference covered sufficiently in theory and training; what is respondents' own place in birth order and which personal issues do they bring to the transference and countertransference relationship.

Respondents were excited to discuss sibling transference and talked about a few aspects of it clearly such as sexuality in sibling transference and the effect of their own birth order on countertransference. However, they generally found it difficult to articulate thoughts, beliefs, and experiences on the topic when questioned. Although respondents believed sibling transference was important, few had received training of any form regarding it.

In respondents clinical work, sibling transference manifested most commonly in the form of competition and envy. Other common forms that difficulties in sibling relationships took in the transference were abuse, caretaking, or parentification.

Many different factors elicited sibling transference, such as age, race, gender, and the demeanor of the therapist, or events in the life of the patient or therapist.

The role of authority in traditional analytic therapy interfered with the development or recognition of sibling transference, unless the patient had an older, authoritative sibling. Most respondents believed a theoretical gap exists regarding sibling transference due to a focus on parents in general, rather than siblings, in theory and literature, and an emphasis in Freudian, psychoanalytic theory on parents, as well as its genesis in a Caucasian, European culture valuing individualism.

Table of Contents

CHAPTER 1

Introduction

Although much has been written in psychoanalytic literature on the topic of transference in psychotherapy, surprisingly little attention has been paid to sibling transference phenomena. While discussion and case material is presented on parental transference in training programs for clinicians, again, there seems to be little information presented on the development or expression of transference related to siblings. This absence raises the question of what might contribute to this apparent oversight. Sisters and brothers can have a tremendous impact on an individual's development, relationships, and current functioning; therefore the lack of attention paid to siblings transference is puzzling.

The definition of transference which will be used in this study was developed by Ogden (1994) who defined transference as "not simply a transferring of one's experience of one's internal objects onto external objects; it is as importantly a transferring of one's experience of the internal environment within which one lives onto the analytic situation" (p. 138). Kornberg's (1965) "totalistic" definition of countertransference as the total emotional reaction of the psychoanalyst to a patient in the treatment situation will be used in this study. Transference and countertransference are understood in this study to form together an intersubjective system of reciprocal mutual influence. These definitions were chosen to allow for a broader conceptualization of these concepts within a relational context, which may be more likely to encompass the variation of meanings which study participants may bring to the topic. Throughout this project, use of the term transference is intended to include countertransference as a related aspect.

If one assumes that siblings do have an impact on the developing individual, it would seem likely that they also play a role in shaping psychological structures and object relations. The traditional and contemporary definitions of transference, do not specify parents as the only source of transference, referring instead to "persons," "important figures," "objects," "feelings," "states of mind." Considering that any important person can contribute to the transference relationship, it seems more than likely that siblings could manifest in the psychotherapy relationship. Looking, then, at siblings in transference, several questions become apparent.

One of the most central questions is whether or not experienced therapists observe the phenomenon of sibling transference in their practices. If therapists do observe sibling transference, what has their experience of it been, and how do they differentiate it from parental transference? This last question is related to the broader inquiry into how sibling transference is conceptualized. If the therapist does have some experience of sibling transference, does it include theory related to their experience? If therapists do not hold their experience of sibling transference in a theoretical framework, either developmental or structural, does this indicate the presence of a theoretical gap regarding this form of transference? If there is such a gap, what might account for it?

When clinicians do report the occurrence of sibling transference, it would be helpful to know if it is experienced as an important aspect of treatment. If it is observed, does this form of transference become more apparent during particular phases of treatment, or under certain circumstances, and how is it elicited?

More particular questions would attempt to ascertain how the age and birth order of the therapist and patient may contribute to sibling transference. The sibling gender and age of the patient and therapist may also interrelate in the formation of this transference. Exploring the therapist's own sense of how their sibling order may impact their own transference or countertransference issues would be meaningful information.

Some authors (Agger, 1988; Bank and Kahn, 1982; Lesser, 1978) have noted the lack of attention to sibling transference in training for analytic work. If there is such a lack in training, it would be meaningful to understand the reasons for this.

Lastly, looking at the role that culture may play in awareness of sibling transference, training, and development of theory related to this issue is relevant. Could it be that an emphasis on parental transference is embedded in a cultural context, which may deny the experience of persons from other cultures?

In this study, I examined the phenomenon of sibling transference, including countertransference, in psychoanalytically oriented treatment. I interviewed 16 therapists using a psychodynamic approach in their practice. I developed an understanding, through the interviews, of the effects that sisters and brothers may have on the development of transference and countertransference in the treatment relationship looking at such factors as how the age, gender, and birth order, of the analyst and patient interrelate. Also explored was these therapists' experience of sibling countertransference. Although it would be interesting to examine the role of culture on therapist's awareness and beliefs regarding sibling transference, it was beyond the scope of this study.

The primary underlying assumption of this study was that sibling transference does exist in adult psychotherapy, and that it has been neglected in both theory and training. The birth order, age, and sex of both therapist and patient were believed to influence the recognition and handling of sibling transference. The psychological relationship of both therapist and patient with siblings in childhood and as adults was thought to affect the sibling transference as well. Difficulties related to siblings, such as sibling birth, loss, or rejection, competition, incest, and displacement manifest in sibling transference. Positive qualities of sibling relationships, such as identification and love, also emerge in the transference. This study was designed to explore these assumptions through qualitative interviews with clinicians experienced with the phenomenon of transference. The information gathered should not only lead to greater definition of the topic, but also facilitate generation of hypotheses regarding sibling transference as well.

It is my hope that gaining further information regarding this particular form of transference will help therapists become more effective in identifying this aspect of the treatment relationship, and more able to utilize their countertransference reactions in a growth enhancing way for themselves and their patients. It is my assumption that paying attention to sibling transference phenomena allows the patient increased possibility of personal development through resolution and growth of internalized sibling object relationships. Gaining knowledge of how experienced clinicians understand and work with sibling transference also provides an important contribution to training programs for psychotherapists in this topic area.

Literature Review

The literature on sibling transference is very scanty. Most references to the topic are anecdotal or theoretical, based on personal experience, informal observation, and case reports of colleagues and the authors. Systematic research of either a qualitative or quantitative nature is absent. I will begin with an overview of the more general topics of transference and countertransference. I will then attempt to present a summary of the writings on sibling transference.

Transference

Freud (1895) first described transference as a source of resistance to the analytic process, based on what he called "a false connection" between the person of the physician and the disturbing ideas which arise from the content of the analysis. Ten years later (1901/1905e/1953) he referred to transference as

> new editions or facsimiles of the impulses and phantasies which are aroused and made conscious during the progress of the analysis; but they have this peculiarity, which is characteristic for their species, that they replace some earlier person by the person of the physician. (p. 116)

He noted that past experiences are revived as applying to the physician in the present and some of these transferences have a content which differs from that of their model in no respect whatever except for the substitution. He later (1909) pointed out that transference arises spontaneously in all human relationships just as it does between the patient and physician. He also stated that transference is not created by psychoanalysis, but that psychoanalysis merely reveals it.

Anna Freud (1936) later defined transference as all impulses experienced by the patient in relation to the analyst which are not newly created by the objective analytic situation, but have their source in early object relations and are merely revived under the influence of the repetition compulsion.

Fenichel (1945) distinguished the more specific transference of the psychoanalytic situation from the more general and universal phenomenon. In everyday life, he felt that it is a general human propensity to interpret one's experience in the light of the past. The more repressed impulses seek expression, and the more difficult it is to correctly evaluate the difference between present and past, the greater the transference component of a person's behavior. In contrast, according to Fenichel, the psychoanalytic situation promotes production of transference in two ways. First, the environment reacted to has a relatively uniform and constant character and therefore the transference component becomes much more pronounced. Second, the analyst provides no actual provocation to the patient and responds to affective outbursts by making the patient aware of their behavior. This makes the transference character of the patient's feelings clearer.

Greenacre (1966) also noted that transference is omnipresent in human relationships and felt that it is based on two essential psychological ingredients. The first is the difficulty of the individual to exist long in emotional isolation. The second is the capacity to shift or transfer patterns of emotional relationships from one person to another, provided there is a connecting link between them. She also felt that transference is rooted in early childhood, but that, in therapy, communication through bodily contact and direct gratification is replaced as much as possible by verbal communication.

Greenson (1967) defined transference as a "distinctive type of object relationship" (p. 151). He added that its main characteristic is that the experiences, which could be "feelings, drives, wishes, fears, fantasies, and ideas or defenses against them" (p. 153), do not truly belong to the person upon whom they are bestowed: "Essentially, the person in the present is reacted to as though he were the person in the past" (p. 152).

An "object" as described by Muir (1989) in psychoanalytic usage has two meanings:

> (a) It is the human figure (or part of that figure) that is invested with instinctual energy. This definition derives from Freud's (1905d) source, aim and object. (b) It can also be the mental representation of the real object.
>
> An internal object relationship is the establishment of an internalized pattern of relationship with an invested object that is evoked repetitively whenever the needs and affects associated with that relationship are mobilized. (p. 49)

Ogden (1986) also provides a definition of transference from the view of internal object relations. He states that "transference can take one of two forms, depending on whether it is the role of the object or that of the self in the internal object relationship that is assigned to another person in the externalization process" (p. 151). The first form of transference occurs when the role of the internal object is projected, and the patient experiences another person as they have unconsciously experienced that internal object (an unconscious split-off part of the ego identified with the object). The second form of transference occurs when the patient experiences another person in the same way the internal object (split-off portion of ego identified with the object) experiences the aspect of the ego identified with self. Ogden (1994) later defined transference as a transferring of one's experience of the internal environment within which one lives onto the analytic situation.

A contemporary conceptualization of transference as an organizing activity is offered by intersubjective theorists, Stolorow, Brandchaft, and Atwood (1987). They understand transference to refer to "all the ways in which the patient's experience of the analytic relationship is shaped by his own psychological structure - by the distinctive, archaically rooted configurations of self and object that unconsciously organize his subjective universe" (p. 36). Transference is seen as an expression of the universal psychological striving to organize experience and create meanings. This reconceptualization of transference as an organizing activity, rather than more simply as a resistance, changes the focus to invite attention to both the patient's psychological structures and the input from the analyst that they assimilate (Wachtel, 1980).

Stone (1995) specifically includes persons other than parents in his object relations definition of transference, which he describes as

> the tendency to repeat, in a current setting, attitudes, feelings, impulses, and desires experienced or generated in early life in relation to important figures in the individual's development. These original figures are primarily the parents but may include other family members or even persons outside the family who have assumed important functional roles in actuality. Sometimes the last may have been invoked for substitutive or defensive reasons; at other times because of their unique actual significance to the subject. (p. 110)

Again, the later definition of transference developed by Ogden (1994) will be used for the purpose of this study, which allows for the inclusion of others, such as siblings, in its broad terms of transferring one's experience of the internal environment onto the analytic situation. (For further discussion of transference, and different aspects of it, see: Bird, 1972; Gill, 1979; Levy, 1984; Szasz, 1963.)

Countertransference.

Countertransference was originally defined by Freud (1910/1957) in the following way:

> We have become aware of the counter-transference which arises in him
> [the analyst] as a result of the patient's influence on his unconscious
> feelings, and we are almost inclined to insist that he shall recognize this
> counter-transference in himself and overcome it. (pp. 144-145)

Therefore, countertransference encompasses all emotions in the therapist that are evoked or provoked by something in the patient that are unresolved issues of the therapist's past.

Winnicott (1949) discussed the idea that countertransference could be a source of information. He classified countertransference phenomena in the following way:

> (1) Abnormality in counter-transference feelings, and set relationships and
> identification that are under repression in the analyst. The comment on this
> is that the analyst needs more analysis, and we believe this is less of an
> issue among psycho-analysts than among psycho-therapists.
> (2) The identifications and tendencies belonging to an analyst's personal
> experiences and personal development which provide the positive setting
> for his analytic work and make his work different in quality from that of
> any other analyst.
> (3) From these two I distinguish the truly objective counter-transference, or
> if this is difficult, the analyst's love and hate in reaction to the actual
> personality and behavior of the patient, based on objective observation.
> (pp. 69-70)

Kernberg (1965) described a "totalistic" definition of countertransference where it is viewed as the total emotional reaction of the psychoanalyst to the patient in the treatment situation" (p. 38).

Ogden (1986) describes two forms of countertransference. One involves the therapist's unconscious identification with that aspect of the patient's ego identified with the object, similar to Racker's concept of complementary identification (1957). The second consists of the therapist's identification with the self-component of the patient's internal object relationships, similar to Racker's (1957) concordant identification.

Blum and Goodman (1995) note that countertransference can sometimes be defined to include the mutual reaction of analyst and analysand to each other's transference in the following way:

> Just as the patient develops a transference to the analyst and the analyst develops a countertransference to the patient's transference, so also the analyst has transferential reactions to the patient, and the patient in turn may have transference reactions to the analyst's countertransference. (p. 121)

Stolorow, Brandchaft, and Atwood (1987) define countertransference as a "manifestation of the analyst's psychological structures and organizing activity" (p. 42). They take the intersubjective position that it has a decisive impact in shaping the transference and codetermining which of its specific dimensions will occupy the experiential foreground of the analysis.

To present an exhaustive and comprehensive literature review of transference and countertransference would be beyond the scope of this study. They are central concepts to all psychodynamically oriented psychotherapies. (For further discussion of countertransference, see: Heimann, 1950; Kernberg, 1965; Little, 1951; Racker, 1972; Reich, 1951; Tower, 1956.) The object relations concept of countertransference, as described by Kernberg (1965) and Ogden (1986) will be used in this study.

Sibling Transference.

In her article, "Psychoanalytic Perspectives on Sibling Relations," Agger pointed out that clinical evidence shows that in adult life, "transference aspects of a predominantly sibling nature may emerge to govern interpersonal relationships, self-concept, ego functioning, and certain phases of psychoanalytic treatment" (1988, p. 4). However, countertransference issues, such as inhibition and anxiety regarding competition and incest, and lack of exposure in both training and personal analyses may cause the therapist to overlook sibling interaction as a silent variable in personality formation, neurosis, and treatment (Agger, 1988). She argued that lack of synthetic work in literature on the subject may also be due to the overestimation of sibling events as belonging to objective reality alone, according to Agger, and commitment to traditional theoretical concepts causes one to focus on parental transference within the oedipal helix.

Bank and Kahn (1982) believe that the "vertical parent-to-child vector is so deeply embedded in dynamic theory that master therapists ignore the parallel, peer-related, horizontal vectors of sibling-to-sibling relationships, and instruct the next generation of therapists in the same manner" (p. 299). Additionally, parent transference, rather than sibling transference, interpretations are inevitable if the therapist views him/herself as parentlike, wise, beneficent, and omnipotent and the patient as childlike, helpless, confused, and dominated by infantile feelings (p. 299).

Lesser (1978) found that an analyst may secretly gratify omnipotent wishes through an authority role and may be loath to acknowledge that the patient may relate to him/her "as one of the kids" (p. 44). If, however, the therapist permits a more sibling like relationship, this will be "more egalitarian, promote faster change, and deny the patient the illusion that he or she can be protected or nurtured interminably" (Bank & Kahn, 1982, p. 300).

Lesser (1978) believes that inattention to feelings and attitudes rooted in sibling relationships can be a source of therapeutic stalemate and failure. She referred to research by Szalita (1968) which found that omission of an important early relationship, usually with a sibling, was one reason for dissatisfaction with previous analyses. Several authors (Agger, 1988; Bank & Kahn, 1982; Lesser 1978) stated that since personal analysis is probably the most important aspect of training for analytic work, inattention to sibling influence tends to be perpetuated.

Bank and Kahn also speculate that another factor which contributes to avoidance of sibling issues by psychotherapists is their birth order position. They point out that many therapists are first-borns and may have experienced "dispossession" of maternal attention by their later-born siblings (1982, p. 301). This might make a first-born therapist have less therapeutic tolerance for younger siblings or for building sibling bonds in therapy.

Therapists at mid-life (thirty-five to fifty-five) may become insensitive to difficult sibling issues of individuals in treatment if they have grown professionally successful and are no longer in active conflict with their own siblings. These therapists may have actively repressed personal memories of conflict-laden years of childhood and adolescence (p. 302).

Ian Graham (1988) believes that psychoanalytic study of sibling issues in treatment "suffers from a contempt of familiarity" in which the imminence of personal, familial, organizational, and clinical associations to the topic make it difficult to reflect upon it spontaneously with sufficient detachment (p. 88). He tracks the resulting overly exclusive emphasis on effects of the primary relationship with the parents and the tendency to relegate siblings to a "real object" model through the work of several major theorists, including Kernberg (1976) and

Kaplan (1978). He contrasts this with Kohut's (1971) appreciation of the impact of sibling relationships on the narcissistic enmeshment with the mother and awareness that the sibling experience can be a major coorganizer, along with the mother's libidinal and aggressive disposition and behaviors, of the child's psychic experience.

Agger (1988) and Lesser (1978) illustrate how Freudian theory was influenced by his avoidance of and ambivalence toward sibling issues. Agger believes that Freud's conceptualization of the Oedipus complex was effected in the following manner:

> The formulation of the Oedipus complex, in addition to its scientific merit, may have served a neurotic need for a cognitive vehicle to which one could attach a disturbing constellation of primitive feelings. To discover incestuous wishes and murderous fantasies toward parents may have been less distressing than to experience them in connection with siblings where the sadistic component and castration anxiety may be more intense. This reconstruction might account for the survivor guilt that Freud often acknowledged which is continually re-experienced when one has "remained in possession of the field" throughout life. (p. 12)

Lesser also explored the fact that the meaning of Guntrip's (1975) sibling loss in early childhood was not explored sufficiently by either of his analysts.

In contrast, Lasky and Mulliken (1988) believe that although Freud treated the sibling experience in an implicit manner, this does not imply neglect or lack of awareness. They believe that Freud's case histories, dream reports, and interpretations offer examples where the presence of the sibling is often a crucial factor in the dynamic picture. Their examples of this include the case of Little Hans (Freud, 1909/1955), where the birth of a sibling is a precipitating factor of a nascent neurosis, and the case of the Wolf Man (Freud, 1918/1955), where the object choice of maturity is seen as a reversal and displacement of an early traumatic sexual object relationship with a sibling which was causal in the formation of a later neurosis. Lasky and Mulliken give another example of Freud's awareness of the importance of siblings in his statement that "Transference is not necessarily bound to mother or father images, but may also proceed from the 'brother imago'" (1912/1958, p. 100).

Colonna and Newman (1983) have presented a detailed review of Freud's writings relating to the sibling experience. Their findings include acknowledgment of rivalrous feelings towards the sibling, the significant impact of the birth of a sibling on sexual curiosity and on the experience of parental affection, and the effect of the sibling on future object choice.

Increased understanding of the intrapersonal significance of sibling relationships leads to appreciation of both their nourishing and pathogenic potential (Agger, 1988). Parens and Saul (1971) believe the role of the sibling is the basis for the range of relationships with peers, partners, playmates, and coworkers. Graham (1988) has found that the nature of sibling attachments may be a better and more immediate indicator of the quality and potential of marital relationships than the more distant and iconic relationships with parents.

Provence and Solnit (1983) have also emphasized the development-promoting aspects of the sibling relationship. They point out that the sibling experience forces one to realize that one is not singular and unique and that this healthy shaking of the narcissistic bubble is a positive part of the adaptation in a normal sibling relationship. Lasky and Mulliken (1988) believe that healthy sibling attachments may favor establishment of capacity for subtle empathic communications and may foster the ability to share indirectly in the experience of the other. The two major areas that are influenced by siblings are identity and object choice, according to these two authors.

In order to explore sibling phenomena, one must shift to what might be called the borderline area, according to Agger (1988), namely, the area of essentially preoedipal issues. She does not elaborate further on why this focus is primarily preoedipal rather than oedipal.

Agger believes that clues to the presence of siblings in the treatment relationship come from subjective data regarding the patient's sibling experience from countertransference responses which lead associatively to critical periods of influence in the patient's background. Significant material usually crystallizes around particular sibling events, such as sibling birth, sibling rivalry, sibling loss, and qualitative issues such as sibling identification and love. The patient's experience of these events is affected by family history, interactional patterns, role induction vulnerability, intrapsychic organization, and unconscious fantasy. One can look for disguised references to siblings at an abstract level in content that suggests incest, parricide, restitution, and atonement. Role diffusion, achievement aversion, and drive inhibition may also be partly determined by sibling dynamics (Agger, p. 6).

In contrast to Agger, Sharpe and Rosenblatt (1994) discuss sibling issues at both the oedipal and preoedipal level in their work on oedipal sibling triangles. They use the term oedipal sibling triangle

> as shorthand to refer to triangular relationships among two siblings and a parent, or among three siblings, that are sufficiently similar to the standard oedipal triad in dynamics and structural elements to warrant their being described as "oedipal-like." Oedipal, in this usage, refers primarily to the developmental level of structuralization and object relations, not to the specific fantasy regarding a parent In employing such terminology, we are not disregarding that the oedipal situation is more than a specific set of interpersonal relations and that it serves as a developmental milestone, wherein a number of complex structures and functions are elaborated. (p. 492)

Sharpe and Rosenblatt found that in families with multiple siblings,

oedipal-like triangles develop among siblings and parents that exhibit many of the characteristics of the oedipal "parental" triangle. These relationships are not solely displacements of parental oedipal constellations, but may exist parallel to and relatively independent of the oedipal "parental" triangle. Sharpe and Rosenblatt believe these relationships can exert definitive influence on the individual's later identifications, choice of adult love object, and patterns of object relating. Unless the therapist is alert to such issues in treatment, these authors believe that significant areas of conflict will likely remain unresolved.

Sharpe and Rosenblatt point out that oedipal-like constellations involving siblings have generally been regarded as defensive displacements from the parental oedipal conflict to avoid the greater threat of parental incestuous fantasies. Although this can occur, Sharpe and Rosenblatt believe that assuming all such constellations represent displacements reflects an error common to psychoanalytic thinking. This error is automatically attributing stereotypical roles to particular family members, e.g., caretaking to parents, unambivalent competition to siblings, etc.. When these roles cross over, instead of acknowledging that each member may play a variety of roles, the variation is explained as "displacement."

In their clinical work, Sharpe and Rosenblatt have observed the presence of equally affectively charged parental and sibling oedipal issues, both in their patient's historical material and in transference manifestations. They believe that

> displacement can hardly be invoked as an explanation when nothing appears to be displaced from the original conflict, which continues with undiminished intensity.

Moreover, transference attitudes toward "big brother", for example, are manifested differently from those toward "big Daddy." A big brother transference will usually entail attitudes of mingled admiration and more openly intense competition, perhaps with some teasing, with the implicit acknowledgment of a common ultimate parental authority over both siblings. A father transference, on the other hand, will usually embody more of an ambivalent submission and rebellion, or at least resentment of a "final authority (p. 494)."

Sharpe and Rosenblatt attempt to distinguish sibling preoedipal and oedipal dynamics in rivalry, idealization and devaluation, fixations, and describe how these dynamics may manifest in treatment. They also point out both similarities and differences in child-parent and sibling oedipal triangles. The differences are noted in the following categories: (1) nature of the replacement fantasy; (2) formal characteristics; (3) intensity and importance in personality development; (4) resolution of the conflicts. One example of difference between child-parent and sibling oedipal triangles is where the competition is between parent and sibling or two siblings and the prize is the exclusive love a sibling. In this case, not only does the fantasy have a sexual component, but the fantasy wish is more realistically attainable than that in the parental oedipal triangle.

Another example of differentiation between child-parent and sibling oedipal triangle is that the

> genesis and course of sibling oedipal triangles also may differ from that of parental oedipal triangles. The older sibling usually begins with unambivalent negative feelings toward the intruding rival (depending on the older one's age), which later become modified by a positive attachment. The child-parent dyad, on the other hand, begins with a primarily positive attachment that is later modified by negative feelings. The younger sibling's oedipal conflicts in relation to older siblings will more likely be experienced in synchrony with the oedipal phases vis a vis parents, while the older sibling's oedipal triangle may emerge later. (p. 503-504)

Sharpe and Rosenblatt point out that oedipal sibling conflicts are often more difficult and complex to resolve than parental oedipal conflicts. Frequently, they find that a crucial sibling may hardly be mentioned, if at all, until years into treatment and long after parental issues have been significantly explored. They note that the analyst, too, may forget about siblings, not only out of theoretical bias, but because of countertransference issues related to personal conflicts with siblings.

Lastly, Sharpe and Rosenblatt believe that difficulty in resolution of oedipal sibling conflict is related to general social and developmental factors. These include: The less strict incest taboo against sexual feelings and activity between siblings makes the child less subject to parental and social pressures to displace or repress such erotic feelings; feeling and tolerating hostility towards one's siblings, while not usually considered desirable, is generally tolerated to a greater degree than expressing hostility toward parents; and acting out of erotic and hostile feelings may then tend to evoke more intense feelings of guilt than were these affects merely expressed in fantasy. In sibling oedipal triangles, the sought-after position of exclusive love seems more realistically achievable to the child and the aim is thus less easily relinquished, whereas in the oedipal struggle with the parents, the rivalry and wish to destroy the existing parental relationship is strongly countered by the wish to retain parents as parents for security and survival. Finally, losing to a sibling who is more of a peer inflicts a more grievous narcissistic injury, according to Sharpe and Rosenblatt.

Ian Graham (1988) discusses sibling transference from an analytical perspective; however, he uses a developmental and structural approach, with the use of some geological terms, to illustrate his ideas. He believes that sibling phenomenology is layered according to the associated object cathexes and the characteristic formations of the infantile neurosis. He finds that the density of this layering is suggested by his experience that conflict-specific developmental sibling object relations are often at considerable variance with the manifest concurrent relationships with the real-life siblings. This requires discriminating between emerging infantile images of the sibling and their impact on current reports of actual sibling behavior. The ultimate clinical features of such a developmental line is eventual alignment of internal and external images of siblings.

Graham (1988) divides sibling object relations into three major categories as they occur in the analysis of transference. The first category is the baseline maternal sibling matrix. This primary sibling environment shows a ring of sibling objects rotating around the primary parental objects in a sequence that varies from the original sibling rank to rankings based, for example, on the popularity with the parents. The patient may restage this primary and internalized environment with "the imminence and potency of the sibling object whose orbits are much closer to us much of the time than are those of the parents of our childhood" (p. 105). The internal analytic work on sibling separation-individuation sequences with its associated attachments, role relationships, and affects, varies according to the sibling profile and its relationship to the patient's experience of the various libidinal and aggressive stages. According to Graham, these interweave with the parallel relationships to the parents and add a richness and complexity to the middle phase of analysis. He believes this is the unique contribution of the sibling transference to the phenomenology of the analysis.

The second category of sibling object relations occurring in analysis of transference is the infantile new sibling configuration impacting on the infantile neurosis. This subsequent event of the new sibling object provides immediate impact and can cause pathology related to the dynamic and adaptive features of these events throughout childhood, adolescence, adulthood, and early middle age.

The third major category, the adaptive and dynamic impact of contemporary adult sibling relationships, has both real and transference impact during the course of analysis. One example Graham provides is the early ambivalence of siblings when one of them goes into analysis, in which the analyst is viewed as much like a new sibling as a new parent.

Graham believes that the multivaried combinations of sibling enmeshment seem to require their own specific form of resolution and atonement in analysis, leading to release from the attachment and an augmented sense of individuation from the sibling, together with formation of new relationships to peers, colleagues, coworkers, partners, and other loved ones. This usually involves separation, not only from the individual, but also from specific assignments and role relationships, such as the polarized complement to a sibling's quality.

Bank and Kahn (1982) find that patients are unlikely to bring up the subject of brothers and sisters on their own, and believe that therefore therapists should always probe a sibling dynamic for its potential to produce strong emotional reactions. These reactions can sometimes appear when the therapist is relatively silent: "The patient may then begin to project the image of loving or sadistic or gentle or hateful brother or sister onto the therapist" (p. 303).

Bank and Kahn note several specific sibling transference reactions. Patients who have an aggressive, compulsive need to compete with the therapist, often have been victims of a destructive sibling's tyranny. Caretaker siblings may essentially hate their position of dependency in therapy. Incestuous siblings may project and re-create, through transference, the old dynamic of secrecy, mistrust, anxiety, and sometimes love of a sibling. Well siblings who stand out in contrast to their disturbed sibling may engage in a reversal in therapy. In this reversal, there is a splitting of good and acknowledged parts from bad and repressed parts. In these cases, the therapist should avoid being the idealized angel that the patient wants also still to be, or the reviled devil that the disturbed sibling was too often seen to be.

Agger (1988) points out the role of sibling imagos and role expectations carried over from the parents' past and maintained in the present family. These can operate as unconscious parental injunctions for the developing child, compelling a child to develop in such a way as to fulfill implicit roles ascribed to it. In addition, Agger believes that borderline parents are especially prone to using the primitive defenses of splitting and projective identification to induce sibling role and conflict behavior among their children to satisfy their own narcissistic needs and to generate destructive patterns of relatedness among them to gratify aggressive inclinations.

When a parent fails to supply empathy, caring, or limit-setting, the child may instinctively turn to a sibling substitute. In this augmented sibling influence, the proper functions of a defense, discharge of affect, reassurance, and disguise, are fulfilled (Agger, 1988). Failure to take cognizance of the specific influence such siblings may exert may lead to inaccurate analysis (Lesser, 1978).

Rosenbaum (1963) has found that sibling rejection or deprivation may have a more traumatic impact on a child than similar experiences in relation to a parent because sibling hatred gives rise to the "most destructive fantasies and impulses human beings possess" (p. 517). In addition, the immaturity of the sibling precludes the operation of inner controls and the tempering force of maternal drives (Lesser, 1978).

Agger (1988) found that patients who were only children often form a positive attachment to the therapist based on the unconscious fantasy that he or she is their long-for confidant and older sibling or their longed-for playmate and younger sister or brother. If these longings are not taken into account, they will endure as a resistance and block further individuation.

She also found that during periods of stress, due either to depressive, hopeless feelings, or, at the other extreme, erotic strivings, a patient may exclaim, "this is too much for us; there's no help anywhere," or, "this is bigger than both of us; why not give in to our sexual attraction?" (p. 28). She interprets these forms of distress as a way to convey a sense of abandonment similar to that felt by sibling pairs left to their own desperate devices.

Erikson's (1950) stage of initiative versus guilt is most affected by pathological variants in the sibling relationship, according to Agger. Conflict experienced between initiative and guilt may determine a lifelong tendency toward being victimized, selecting only aim-inhibited relationships, and seeking the shadow of another's stronger personality.

If a sibling death occurs before a child's birth, the conscious expectation of the family that the child will be a replacement for the lost child preempts the significance of unconscious fantasy as a formative factor. In older children, the death, injury, or impairment of a sibling might generate a pathological mourning reaction which exerts a lifelong critical effect on self-image, behavior, use of aggression, and treatment outcome. When this occurs, the internalization of such a fantasized commission of a preoedipal crime is difficult to unearth and demonstrate through traditional therapeutic methods (Agger, 1988).

Most importantly, Agger believes that although countertransference responses within the therapist-patient mutual interaction are good indicators of sibling influence, care should be taken in formulating interpretations because the degree of one's own self-awareness may be particularly murky in this dyadic area. However, when there is successful attention to anxiety regarding sibling issues, relief ensues and relief from guilt regarding sibling fantasies of parricide and incest may be followed by feelings of atonement through the severance of primitive ties and the subsequent development of the capacity for novel relationships in the here-and-now. Lesser (1978) believes that the analyst who works productively cannot be limited to one role, but must allow her/himself to be transformed into a sibling as well as a parent, sometimes both simultaneously.

Daniel Coleman (1996), in his recent work on positive sibling transference, noted that developments of collaborative and post-modern psychoanalytic therapies make sibling transference more recognizable and understandable, in contrast to a parent-child transference model reflecting the "paternalistic, positivist assumptions of traditional psychoanalysis" (p. 377). One of his examples of sibling transference follows:

> In my example of therapists using the words "Mom" and "Dad" to identify the parents in their client-families, I stated that this linguistic practice revealed the therapists' sibling transferences. . . . Generally a harmless identification with the child, this becomes problematic when the client's "Mom" and "Dad" become projective bearers of confused feelings about the therapist's own parents. (p. 378)

Coleman believes that positive sibling transference is the foundation relational dynamic in the psychotherapy practiced by many contemporary psychotherapists. Although it is one of an infinite variety of transference, according to Coleman, it is the one induced by the "working alliance" at the onset and it is the equilibrium returned to in the working through of more intense and problematic transferences. The positive sibling transference provides a transference based understanding of the working alliance.

In another interesting example of sibling transference, Coleman notes that

> Winnicott, in a sibling moment, once stated that he interpreted so that the client would not think that he knew too much (Phillips, 1988)! This showing of one's humanity encourages a peer-sibling transference rather than a parental transference. This approach also reflects a therapist preference for a sibling-like relationship, one of those therapist transference issues which tends to become invisible. (1996, p. 379)

Coleman also notes that there are many examples of sibling transference relationships outside of therapy where the healthy responsiveness of the transference sibling varies. Interestingly, he points out that gang phenomena may be an example of a sibling fantasy gone awry.

There are several articles which are more specialized or applied in the topic area of sibling transference. The areas which these articles discussed included: sibling transference issues during a therapist's pregnancy (Appelbaum, 1988; McGarty, 1988), the role of siblings in analytic group psychotherapy (Rabin, 1989), the effect of internalized siblings on a sense of being good in late adolescents (Balsam, 1988), and a case illustration of a delusional merger with a brother (Stolorow & Stolorow, 1989).

In summary, there does exist some literature about sibling transference. Most of the authors conclude that this form of transference does exist and can have an important role in psychotherapy. They also tend to agree that it has been neglected in training programs and theory development for a number of reasons. Little of the information in the articles reviewed, however, was systematically collected or complete, and most accounts were anecdotally derived from clinical experience. This study attempted to develop further understanding of sibling transference and countertransference, to generate hypotheses, and explore in greater depth the therapist's experience of this aspect of treatment.

CHAPTER 2

Method

Introduction

The quasi-phenomenological method was used for this study. Sixteen

respondents were interviewed regarding their understanding and experience of

sibling transference. The participants were psychotherapists practicing from a

psychoanalytic, preferably object relations theoretical orientation. Using subjects

with this theoretical approach was critical for the investigation of transference and

countertransference, which are central to the psychoanalytical approach.

Respondents had practiced psychotherapy, post license, for at least five years.

This allowed for adequate experience in the field to observe transference

phenomena.

Although the sample was small, an attempt was made to include some

variation of gender, race, age, and birth order to permit some data analysis from

different vantage points in these domains. Recruitment was conducted through the

professional referral network of myself and colleagues. Flyers were also

submitted to professional organizations of therapists who met the criteria stated

above.

Respondent Characteristics

The sixteen respondents ranged in age from 40 to 62 years old. It was more

difficult to find men who were willing to participate in the study; of the sixteen

respondents only three were male. Two of the respondents were

African/Americans and the remainder were Caucasian. Attempts to recruit Hispanic and Asian respondents were unsuccessful. Ten of the respondents had earned doctorates, and nine of those held clinical psychology licenses. Five others were licensed Marriage, Family, and Child Counselors (MFCC), and one was a licensed clinical social worker (LCSW). All of the respondents had at least five years of experience doing psychotherapy under their licenses. One of the male respondents had practiced under both his MFCC license and his certificate as a Rehabilitation Counselor (CRC). The years of experience ranged from five to 36 years.

There was variation in the birth order of the respondents. Seven of them were first of multiple sibling groups, ranging from one sibling to six siblings. Six of them were second born of either one or two siblings. Three were the youngest of multiple siblings groups of three, six, and nine. One respondent was an only child, and one was a female of a male/female twin pair which had one older brother. Please refer to Table 1 for an illustration of birth order and gender demographics.

The majority of the respondents attempted to answer all items of the questionnaire. There were a few respondents who elected to skip a small number of items which they felt they could not answer adequately due to lack of experience or training in the subject area. There were numerous occasions when respondents gave illustrations of sibling dynamics or issues, but failed to articulate how these appeared in transference or countertransference. The responses of the respondents within the six main topic areas are summarized in the results section of this study.

Table 1.

Respondents' Demographics

Subject	M/F	Race	Age	License	Yrs. Exp.	Birth Order
1	F	Cauc.	50	LCSW	23	2nd of 2 (b,g)
2	F	Cauc	50	Ph.D., MFCC	6	2nd of 2 (b,g)
3	F	Cauc.	49	PSY	15	2nd of 3 (b,g,b)
4	F	Cauc.	49	LCSW	16+	1st of 2 (g.b)
5	M	Cauc.	47	PSY	13	1st of 4 (b,b,b,b)
6	F	Cauc.	49	PSY	10	1st of 3 (g,g,g)
7	F	Cauc.	40	MFCC	5-1/2	2nd of 3 (g,g,g)
8	F	Cauc.	50	PSY	20	2nd of 2 (b,g)
9	F	Cauc.	52	PSY	19	1st of 6, 4 bro./1 sis
10	F	Cauc.	47	MFCC	15	2nd of 3 (b,g,g)
11	F	Cauc.	48	PSY	8	Only child
12	F	Cauc.	50	PSY	5	Twin (b-g,b)
13	F	Afr./Amer	62	PSY	36	9th of 9 (4b, 5g)
14	F	Cauc.	48	PSY	16+	1st of 3 (g,b,g)
15	M	Cauc.	52	MFCC, CRC	9	3rd of 3 (g,g,b)
16	M	Afr./Amer	45	MFCC	12	6th of 6 3sis/2bro.

Measures and Procedures

The interview was the method used to gather data in this study. The value of the interview as a qualitative measure is expressed by Belenky, Clinchy, Goldberger, and Tarule (1986) in their classic, Women's Way of Knowing.

> Connected knowing builds on the subjectivists' conviction that the most trustworthy knowledge comes from personal experience rather than the pronouncements of authorities. ... Connected knowers develop procedures for gaining access to other people's knowledge. At the heart of these procedures is the capacity for empathy. Since knowledge comes from experience, the only way they can hope to understand another person's ideas is to try to share the experience that has led the person to form the idea. (p. 113)

The open-ended, clinical interview method was chosen for this study to allow for more depth, flexibility, and broader coverage of this topic. This was thought to enhance the generation of hypotheses about sibling transference. The interview method allows the practitioner to reflect on this subjective experience and "when someone reflects-in-action, he becomes a researcher in the practice context" (Schon, 1983, p. 68).

Being a female researcher, the qualitative methods which explore and believe what feels real to the subject enhances an experience which Belenky, et al. (1986) believe is important to women, "perhaps because it is founded upon genuine care and because it promises to reveal the kind of truth they value - truth that is personal, particular, and grounded in firsthand experience" (p. 113).

The interview approach began with the area of study, sibling transference, and what is relevant to that area was allowed to emerge. This is the basis for "grounded theory," as defined by Strauss and Corbin (1990, p. 23) which is inductively derived from the study of the phenomenon it represents. According to these researchers, qualitative methods, such as the interview, have an advantage "when trying to uncover the nature of persons' experiences with a phenomenon . . . and can be used to uncover and understand what lies behind any phenomenon about which little is yet known" (p. 19). This makes the qualitative method particularly helpful for the study of sibling transference which is a phenomenon about which little is known at this time. Additionally, qualitative methods "can give intricate details of phenomena that are difficult to convey with quantitative methods" (Strauss and Corbin, p. 19) and thereby add to the richness of the data gathered in this project.

The subjects in this study were interviewed using an open-ended, semi-structured interview schedule (see Appendix A). The interview began with open ended questions designed to explore their knowledge and experience of sibling transference. The questions then became more focused to obtain more complete and specific data which may not have been included in their answers to the open-ended questions. The interview schedule was designed to elicit general information about the respondents' awareness of sibling transference and countertransference, theory, and more particular data on its prevalence, timing, and interaction with age, gender, and therapist training. Respondents who agreed to participate in the study were mailed the interview schedule prior to the interview. This allowed them time to reflect on their experience with the topic, so that they may be better prepared to offer information regarding their experience, ideas, or theory on the topic. Respondents could choose not to respond to any questions if they wished during the interview process.

The interviews were tape recorded and transcribed. The transcripts were the material used for data analysis.

Treatment of the Data

After the interviews were transcribed, they were analyzed for thematic content. Care was taken not to alter the original material. The transcripts were read multiple times to identify trends and themes associated with sibling transference and countertransference, and to address the particular questions asked. The themes and data presented were then analyzed for content and frequency across the study.

CHAPTER 3

Results

Introduction

This study investigated sibling transference and countertransference in psychotherapy with adults. The findings organized well thematically around six main topics. The first topic looked at how sibling transference and countertransference might manifest in psychotherapy. This included general, exploratory information regarding whether and how the therapist had experienced this form of transference, and what might have triggered the development of such transferences.

The second topic area looked more closely at specific variables which contribute to the manifestation of sibling transference. The specific variables explored included the interrelationship of age and gender, specific attributes of sibling relationships, and how these could contribute to sibling transference and countertransference. This topic also included attention to how sexuality in sibling relationships might manifest in the transference. The third topic, still addressing factors contributing to the development of sibling transference, explored the impact and role of the therapist's authority in the psychotherapy relationship on the development and/or recognition of sibling transference.

The fourth topic area looked more closely at the analytic dynamics of sibling transference by trying to understand how the therapist might differentiate sibling transference from parental transference. Experiences when sibling transference might have served as a resistance to other forms of transference were explored. Conversely, therapists also described cases in which some other form of transference may have served as a resistance to sibling transference.

The fifth topic area looked at the inclusion in or exclusion from sibling transference in psychoanalytic theory and training. Therapists related their beliefs regarding whether or not a theoretical gap exists about sibling transference and, if there is such a gap, what might account for it. They also described any professional training they may have received on sibling transference. They assessed the importance of sibling transference in treatment, and how awareness of this form of transference might affect treatment.

The sixth topic area looked more at the person of the therapist in terms of birth order, and possible transference issues in regard to siblings. All were asked, if possible, to relate their awareness of such transference issues and countertransference to experiences in their work.

Topic 1 - How sibling transference and countertransference manifest in treatment. General experiences of sibling transference.

The inquiry into the first topic area began by asking respondents if they had experienced sibling transference, and, if so, what thoughts, feelings, verbalizations, or actions occurred which made them feel it might be sibling transference. All of the respondents believed that they may have experienced it in some form or another. They provided case examples to illustrate how and when it occurred in their practices.

They reported experiencing sibling transference in numerous ways. These included patient's experience with the therapist of competition, rivalry, envy, jealousy, narcissistic wounds such as feeling judged or criticized, caretaking by a patient who was a caretaker for siblings, in sadomasochistic parts of the transference when that had been part of the experience with a sibling, expectation of help that patients had received from an older sibling, experiences of merger, playfulness, and love which was experienced with siblings. Table 2 on the following page summarizes their responses.

The most predominant theme mentioned where sibling transference was experienced by patient's was related to competition. Nine respondents described patient's experience of sibling transference through issues of competition with the therapist, and related issues of envy, jealousy, and rivalry. One therapist expressed it as "competition or envy that has to do with being peers, an identification with me that does not feel like I am being idealized, something else is going on" (* #3).

Another therapist said that she has felt competition in the therapy when a patient was looking at professions, and started talking about the work she did. This

Table 2.

Responses to General Inquiry of Experience with Sibling Transference

---

* Number given in quote refers to the respondent's number from Table 1.

Frequency of Response	Respondent #	Topic Mentioned
9	1,2,3,4,7, 11,12,13,14	Appearing as Competition (*5), Envy (3), Jealousy (2), or Rivalry (2) in transference. (*Frequency)
4	2,5,7, 12	Patient caretaking in therapy as did with siblings.
3	10,5,7	Occurring when parents have been absent, or neglectful.
3	13,15,16	Transferring positive feelings towards sibling to therapist i.e. love, playfulness, trust.
3	1, 6, 12	Kohut, twinship transference.
2	13, 15	Discussed sibling countertransference.
1	14	Sense of entitlement in transference of only children.
1	8	Difficulty with trust with therapist if difficult trusting sibling.
1	10	Sexual abuse by siblings in transference.
1	3	Fantasy or phantom sibling in transference.
1	3	General identification with therapist as sibling.
1	4	Patient feeling judged or criticized , narcissitically wounded in therapy as they were with sibling.

therapist sees a number of psychotherapists in her practice, and she felt that this could contribute to sibling transference.

One respondent gave an example of competition, taken into consideration with birth order and history with siblings. She felt that a female patient who had an older brother that stuttered sometimes seemed to be feeling sorry for her. It appeared to this therapist that the woman was experiencing her as her brother, and would feel badly if she was understanding something before the therapist was, in terms of understanding or ideas.

One case example where a patient demonstrated sibling transference in competition in the treatment was a woman/man who felt inferior to a very successful sibling, and who also felt inferior to her therapist. Another therapist saw women in treatment who felt that she was the kind of daughter that their mothers would have wanted, a "sort of phantom sibling transference" (#9).

Another respondent pointed out that some of her patients feel that there isn't enough of her to go around, and that if they are successful, it means that others cannot be. This therapist also noticed that patients who are only children feel, in relation to other patients, that they own her and the office. The other patients don't seem to exist in their minds. She believed that their transference included a complete sense of ownership of her, that they didn't have to share.

Another theme that was repeated by four respondents was caretaking by patients who had been in caretaking roles with siblings. One therapist cited the case of a woman who had felt responsible for a younger brother who had committed suicide. Another therapist discussed a female patient who became enraged whenever a new person joined her therapy group. This patient was the oldest in a large, abusive family. She felt responsible for new group members, and also felt that there was less emotional space available for her.

In terms of experiences of sibling transference related to themes other than competition and caretaking, three respondents reported experiencing it with patients whose parents were absent and neglectful. One therapist described a woman with several older brothers, two of whom had sexually abused her. The therapist experienced a sadomasochistic quality entering the transference where she was experienced as a brother whenever the patient attempted to control and/or felt dominated by this therapist. The patient sometimes threw her head back with a lot of pain in her neck. The therapist felt that this could be related to the patient's experience of a brother who had forced oral sex on her.

Three therapists mentioned Kohut (1971) and the concept of twinship transference as related to sibling transference. One of these therapists has worked with several twins in her practice. When she is working with a twin who is a woman, she said that it can feel like a twinship transference. These women patients feel very close to their twins, like a "two-headed person" (#6), and it comes out in transference as a kind of merger.

Two therapists described their countertransference experiences in relation to the patient's transference. The first described a patient who transferred feelings towards a deceased, older sister who helped her with difficulties, onto the therapist. The therapist, who was the youngest in a large family, likes to be looked at in that way. The second therapist noticed that when women patients described their relationships with their sisters, it would trigger memories for him. When he first met his own therapist, she reminded him of his older sister, and it felt comforting and reassuring. He felt it helped him make a positive transference to his therapist.

Positive aspects of sibling relationships, such as love, trust, and playfulness, and transfer of these feelings to the therapist were reported by three respondents. The only African/American male therapist reported that some patients will say "you remind me of my brother" (#16); and that this is more likely with African/American patients. If they have a lot of male siblings, they seem more comfortable with him, and sibling transference can look like playfulness. His experience is that siblings are rarely volunteered in discussion by patients, but if they come up when talking with him, it's usually positive.

One respondent mentioned the influence of Alfred Adler on her interest in sibling dynamics in therapy. She believed the notion of sibling transference may really have started with Adler's idea that every child is born into a different family, and that birth order is crucial in development of personality.

Another therapist believed she may have experienced sibling transference with a patient, but did not think she could draw a strict correlation between the relationship with the patient's sibling and the patient's response to her. This respondent questioned the traditional definition of transference, preferring more differentiated formulations of her experience with patients to overarching ideas.

Another therapist summarized nicely how she relates to the concept of sibling transference:

I ask myself, who am I to this person now, including ghosts in the nursery up to present parties, so it could include siblings. I don't separate it out, but look at the spectrum of who I am to the person now, and one possibility is sib, whether they have one or not. So it's not necessarily historical, it could be fantasy, because people without a father still have paternal transference, so this could be true for sibs. So yes, I deal with it, but I had to think about pulling it out and making it a separate category. (#3)

Factors that elicit or contribute to the development of sibling transference

The second, more focused, question relating to the topic of how sibling transference might manifest in treatment asked what might elicit or trigger such a transference. This could include certain events, interpretations, stages of therapy, or other factors. Most of the respondents had ideas regarding what might contribute to sibling transference. Some of their ideas overlapped with their responses to the first question and the following topic area which asked more directly about particular factors. Their ideas are summarized in Table 3.

Most therapists mentioned only one or two possible factors. Only seven responded to the query regarding stage of therapy as a possible factor. Three of the respondents stated possible manifestations of sibling transference, such as envy toward the therapist, but failed to address what might contribute to the development or elicit this form of sibling transference.

The most predominant factors, mentioned by at least four therapists, included: (a) sibling transference evoked by anything in the therapy that reminded the patient of sibling relationships or evoked sibling experience, (b) that it was triggered like any other form of transference, (c) stage of therapy, and (d) the general appearance or characteristics of the therapist, such as a regional accent or mannerisms.

The ideas touched on by at least three therapists included: (a) events in the patients life, such as the illness or death of a sibling, (b) how conflicted or unresolved the patients feelings are regarding a sibling, (c) the family of origin structure and functioning, (d) how sibling countertransference might be evoked if the patient reminds the therapist of a sibling or may not be recognized by an only child therapist, and (e) the race of the patient and therapist.

Table 3.

Factors Eliciting or Contributing to the Development of Sibling Transference

Frequency of Response	Respondent #	Factor Mentioned
7	1, 3, 4, 10, 16, 7, 14	By anything reminding patient of sibling relationship or evoked sibling experience.
4	2, 5, 6, 9	Stages of therapy: a. any, fluid
1	1	b. beginning
2	1,3	c. ending
4	3, 6, 12, 16	Triggered like any other form of transference.
4	1, 6, 10, 11	General appearance, personal characteristics of therapist i.e. regional accent, gestures
4	12, 15, 11, 13	Countertransference evoked if patient or relationships reminds therapist of a sibling, or only child therapist having difficulty recognizing sibling transference.

3	3, 6,11	Patient's life events, i.e. illness or death of sibling
3	5,10,13	Family of origin structure and functioning i.e. only child, sibling dominance, or abusive sibling.
3	1, 6, 14	How conflicted or unresolved patient is regarding sibling.
3	1, 4, 9	Respondent named manifestation of sibling transference, but not what evoked it.
3	12, 13, 16	Race of patient and therapist
2	2, 6	Age of patient and therapist
2	5, 13	The general tone of the therapy relationship
2	5, 13	Focusing on the sibling relationship in therapy
1	16	If the therapist has siblings, more likely to name as contributing to the transference.
1	11	Setting limits, i.e. saying no to patient request
1	2	Profession of patient i.e. if also a therapist.
1	9	Events in therapist's life i.e. illness, physical changes
1	6	Gender of patient and therapist
1	1	Length of treatment, if long term & sibling was important, more likely to occur.

Stage of therapy was one of the two most predominant themes, mentioned by seven respondents, however this was in response to a direct question regarding it as a factor. Two of the seven felt that they could not make a generalization about the effect of stages or had awareness of such an effect. Four of the respondents believed sibling transference could appear at any stage. One therapist stated "not that there are specific stages, but there would be manifestations of it at each stage, any stage, for example, when someone first comes, there may be idealization and envy" (#9). Another respondent believed that sibling transference is fluid, comes and goes, but not any particular phase. He noticed that in the beginning of treatment it could appear with comfort due to familiarity based on resemblance: "I think I like this therapist," or in the end phase in unfinished ways, such as "I dealt with a lot of stuff . . . with feelings about my brother. My feelings about my sister still seem to be unresolved" (#5).

Another therapist with a pronounced regional accent, believed that she experiences sibling transference at the beginning of treatment when patients first notice her accent and try to connect by talking about a relative who lived in that region, memories of having visited the region, or by saying something positive about the region or accent. She also believed that patients somehow make her more like themselves as they terminate, which could be a form of sibling transference. Another therapist reported experiencing sibling transference during the ending stage of therapy, "as you de-idealize and move to end" (#3). She stated that the ending stage brings up fantasies of moving to other relationships with more equality and less authority, like siblings in a family.

The other most predominant factor eliciting sibling transference, mentioned by seven therapists, was anything that evoked sibling relationship experiences. One example of this was given by a therapist who noted envy and competition as a manifestation of sibling transference evoked when a patient sees another patient in the waiting room, or notices an object missing from her office.

Another therapist gave an examples of ways her own behavior could evoke sibling transference. She inquired about money in the case of a woman with an abusive older brother and the patient "had the feeling that I was trying to get things out of her, like what her older brother did . . . that would provoke some of the controlling, who is in charge of what here" (#10). One respondent noticed that when she had to set limits, such as saying no to a patient when they wanted something she couldn't do, it could set up a sibling transference.

In addition to regional accent, three other therapists mentioned the general appearance or demeanor of the therapist as contributing to sibling transference. One example was gestures or mannerisms the therapist might make which reminded the patient of a sibling.

The effect of the therapist on the development of sibling transference was summarized by a therapist in the following way:

> Whatever way the therapist may consciously or unconsciously contribute to that (sibling transference) by certain kinds of age, demeanor, gender, and so may elicit those kinds of things, or the kind of relationship that the therapist may participate in may in some way recreate some kind of sibling relationship...may elicit something similar to what they have experienced. (R. #6)

Another therapist also mentioned that the concrete factors of age and profession are important. She stated that "when they (patients) are close in age to me, or their profession is the same as mine, or close to mine, or if they suspect I have the same marital status, or children the same age as their child's age . . . (they) may have competitive feelings, or they will be more critical or judgmental, and that feels more sibling than parental" (#2)

Three respondents discussed race as a variable when asked about general factors effecting sibling transference. One therapist said that she trained with an

African/American woman who told her that her own experience with African/American women was that they had a desire to merge with her, that they had an expectation of alikeness and sameness that could be a hindrance.

Four respondents spoke of how sibling relationships could manifest in countertransference. One therapist believed that countertransference issues with siblings are likely to get activated if the treatment replicates a situation that closely ties to the therapist's own family and relationship with siblings. Another said that he had experienced it when hearing stories about the patient's life and history that were familiar or similar to his own sibling experiences. One therapist experienced countertransference as sometimes enjoying a kind of sharing that one might like to have with a close sibling. The respondent who was an only child believed that her difficulty trying to put herself in someone's place, but not really knowing what it is like to have a sibling, could be a sibling countertransference.

Three therapists pointed out that certain kinds of unresolved issues, fixations, or important events that have to do with sibling relationships, such as the illness of a sibling, could contribute to sibling transference. One male therapist gave the example of a female patient whose brother committed suicide, who probably experienced him in therapy as the brother she never got to grow up with. Another respondent believed that the death of a parent or illness in a sibling could trigger sibling transference.

Another predominant idea, mentioned by four therapists, was that sibling transference could be triggered like any form of transference, that "it has to do with projections of unresolved issues onto the therapist" (#6). One of these

therapists stated that it occurs

> . . . like any other transference, things that happen in the interchange, or an interpretation that hits the spot, in either direction, transference or countertransference, . . . anything that would remind you in a way, or some aspect of reliving some component of sibling relationships, real or fantasy. (#3)

Another therapist also believed that sibling transference would be elicited by the

same things that elicit other forms of transference. He also believed when the

therapist knows that the patient has siblings, it can trigger the therapist to name

siblings as contributing to the transference.

The effect of family of origin structure and functioning was cited by three

therapists as contributing to sibling transference. Respondent 13 stated that the

patient being an only child or coming from a "family deficit" where there are all

boys, or all girls, could have an impact on their relationship with the therapist.

Another therapist who also believed that sibling transference depends on

the patient's relationships with sibling and family structure stated that she

generally works through parental transference and then becomes aware of sibling

transference, but that it is different when there has been a dominant sibling. In the

case, for example, where an abusive older brother or sister raised the family, it can

come up as caretaking and abusive transference by the patients.

Another respondent pointed out that if a patient has a traumatic history with

a sibling, some interaction that recreates a part of that relationship will trigger a

sibling transference. He used the example of coming late for a session which could bring up feelings of abandonment or betrayal the patient may have experienced with a sibling. In general, several therapists believed that if there were a lot of conflict or unresolved issues with siblings, this would come up in the transference, and that focusing on the sibling relationship in general contributes to it coming up as transference.

In a related theme, one therapist stated that she believed that the extent to which the sibling is an important internal object and how the siblings are represented growing up is an important factor. She also believed that if the patient focused on the parent, and the relationships with the siblings were healthy, then siblings play a less prominent role in the treatment. If the patient brings survivor guilt related to siblings into the treatment, it can be expressed by being "anxious about getting goodies from me, and this has to by undone (by the patient)"(#14).

Two therapists believed that sibling transference could be elicited by the relationship with and very being of the therapist, and that some therapies are more like sibling relationships. One therapist noted that events that happen in the life of the therapist could contribute to sibling transference. She used the example of a patient's knowledge about an illness of the therapist which they have learned about through the grapevine. She felt that any event that brings the therapist into the public eye, personal or professional visibility, could elicit sibling transference, particularly if the patient is in the same profession. She also believed that any physical changes in the therapist, such as appearance or getting more physically fit, could elicit sibling transference.

Topic 2 - Specific variables which might effect sibling transference.

Interrelationship of Age and Gender

Although some respondents brought in age and gender as factors which could elicit sibling transference, as noted in previous examples, all were asked more specifically to address their experience of these concrete factors in the next inquiry on this first topic.

Gender. When asked how sibling gender and therapist gender interrelate in sibling transference, responses ranged from basically no effect, namely, that transference crosses gender, to responses stating it was an important variable. However, the majority of the respondents believed that gender did have some effect. Only two respondents believed it had no effect. One of these respondents said that "it would transfer, for example, if a patient can have transference of either parent with you, it (sibling transference) could happen in the relationship, whatever the sex of the sibling" (#11). The second therapist said that gender was immaterial; being a female therapist, for example, that "doesn't stop the patient from having a paternal or fraternal transference, or others . . . mentors, idealized figures, or hated figures, et cetera, with you" (#9). How the respondents fell in their differing categories is noted in Table 4.

Nine respondents expressed the predominant belief that gender was an important factor and six believed that it had the potential to be an important variable in the development of sibling transference. The nine who believed it was important gave examples from their own psychotherapy experiences and their work with patients.

Table 4.

The effect of sibling and therapist gender on development of sibling transference.

Frequency of response	Respondent #	Effect of Sibling and Therapist Gender on Sibling Transference
2	9, 11	No effect.
5	3, 6, 8, 10, 14	Sibling transference can cross gender line, but gender match can contribute to sibling transference.
9	1, 2, 4, 5, 7, 12, 13, 15, 16	Gender match is important in the development of sibling transference.

One female therapist related a case from her practice of a female patient who had a transference with her in which she felt like the patient's imaginary friend or sister. Another therapist expressed her belief that transference is not genderless and ageless and she reported, for instance, that when she sees a man who has a sister, this man will attribute more to her from his relationship with his sister. One respondent gave an example of a patient who had an abusive brother and an abusive father who was a psychiatrist. She sensed that this patient, who has a positive transference with her because she is female, would have a difficult and different transference relationship with a male therapist.

Another female therapist who believed gender is an important factor said that she saw a lot more sibling transference with female patients. She has a woman in her practice who has just one brother who got all the attention and privileges, and who was very successful at everything. Her mother was depressed and absent. This patient will become very competitive with the therapist, and then the therapist begins to feel a lot of hate and rage. This therapist believes that the sibling transference has crossed gender to her as a female therapist, and that internal states in relation to the brother get projected onto her.

Of those therapists who believed that gender was important, one pointed out that the effect of therapist and patient gender would vary. The therapist could represent something closer to the experience with a sibling, and it could be a big issue, or could represent something very different from the sibling, and then gender may not be as evocative.

One male respondent expressed the idea that the gender relationship in sibling transference depended on family configuration and history. He believed that he could remind someone of a sister if he had certain attitudes, but that it was more likely that he would remind someone of a brother. In general, he thought that cross gender transference could be complicated by sexual tensions. He also thought that cross gender sibling relationships are often as comfortable as one can get with the other gender if it is a good relationship, that it can be more intimate than with either parent, or even adult partners. Another male therapist stated that he was more comfortable himself working with a female therapist because of his connection with his older sister.

Five respondents believed transference can cross gender lines and come up regardless of the gender match, but that sibling gender could contribute to the likelihood that sibling transference would develop. One of these therapists stated that reality intrudes into the work, is a part of it, and a therapist who is the same gender as the patient, or has qualities of the sibling, real or imagined, will elicit those kinds of relationships. Another therapist said that the gender match may not matter a lot in the specifics, but would to the extent that it matters in the real world. Her example was a patient who had a difficult relationship with a brother. This patient had difficulty with men in general and a false sense of safety with women. But she felt that this would fade, and that the "nasty, abusive, or adored brother will get acted out" (#14).

Age. Eight of the respondents believed age could be a factor in the development of sibling transference. Six others believed it could be a factor, but not necessarily. Some of those who believed age was clearly a factor said that the more closely the age match between therapist and patient to that of the patient and sibling, the more likely sibling transference will develop.

Two people believed that if the age gap is very wide between patient and sibling, parental transference or some other form of transference is more likely to develop. Two therapists said that they are getting more parental transference from patients as they age. One of these respondents thought that a patient's "initial take" in therapy can develop depending on age, and that some tranferences are harder to have at different ages. For example, a therapist can say some things to patients when they are older that they can't say when they are a younger therapist.

Another therapist believed that the age match with a sibling could be an advantage or disadvantage. She is an older therapist, age 62, who has worked extensively with grandmothers who are raising their grandchildren. She believed these women related to her age and to the fact that she was also black.

Of the six respondents who believed age could be a factor, but not necessarily, the following therapist is representative in her statement that it makes sense to her that sibling and therapist age would interrelate in effecting sibling transference:

> . . . but, because of the timelessness of the unconscious, it makes no sense at all. It hasn't been relevant or come up in my personal experience. It's quite conceivable that unconsciously in a countertransferential way it could, for example, I could behave toward some patients in a way that is kind of big sister like or whatever. So it may be a little bit invisible to me, I haven't   seen the age issue. (#9)

Another therapist believed age is a real factor in the same way as gender and appearance, and could contribute to the transference, particularly if the therapist has the same qualities as a sibling. However, she also believed that in the unconscious these factors may have no meaning at all, and that transference can happen no matter what the age difference or gender.

Two respondents thought that age was not as important as gender as a contributing factor in sibling transference. One of these therapists stated that if the therapist is close in age to the sibling, there is more likely to be sibling transference; this however, would depend on other characteristics of the siblings as well. She also pointed out that the therapist can become a sibling even when there is a large age difference or when the patient has been the only child. The second therapist believed that whether age contributed to sibling transference depended on the style of the therapist.

Difficulties particular to sibling relationships.

The next area of inquiry into the topic of how sibling transference and countertransference might manifest looked at how specific attributes of sibling relationships could contribute negatively and positively to sibling transference. Their responses are summarized in Table 5.

Table 5.

Difficulties in sibling relationships which may impact sibling transference.

Frequency of Response	Respondent #	Difficulty Mentioned
11	1, 3, 4, 5, 6, 7, 10, 12, 13, 14	Competition, sibling rivalry, envy
5	3, 9, 10, 11, 15	Caretaking or parentification
4	2, 5, 8, 10	Abuse or trauma between siblings

First therapists were asked if there are difficulties particular to sibling relationships that might manifest in sibling transference. Competition, again, was a predominant theme, stated by eleven, the majority of the respondents. One therapist provided a good summary of some of their statements regarding competition as a factor:

and

> There's several; older siblings always stuck caring for a younger sibling are resentful, competition among siblings. There's a sense of the sibling as the favored child which can sometimes feel like a third person in the room. There's the guilt of being favorite. All the Oedipal configurations that lead to favorites that feels conflictual, and survivor's guilt related to that. (#3)

If the patient had a sibling who "was a little bit older, wiser, or more confident" (#6), this could easily manifest in the transference, according to another respondent.

In a related theme, five of the respondents mentioned caretaking and parentification as difficulties in sibling relationships that could be expressed in the transference. One respondent related a case where a patient is an older sister. She felt responsible for her younger siblings, and acted a parent toward the therapist. In the therapy relationship with her, it seemed difficult to have a more equal sibling relationship. Another respondent related a case from her group work where a woman who was an older sister had difficulty whenever new members were added to the group. She would become enraged and anticipated that she was going to have to be responsible in some way for the new member in a way similar to her experience in her family.

One therapist described an interesting case of a female patient whose relationship with her brother, a fraternal twin, illustrates the effect of a difficult sibling relationship on adult development:

I don't think there is any question that this experience with this brother seriously effects her relationships to men. . . . it's not as if . . . the father or mother was irrelevant. But I think there was a way in which this brother was really a force to be dealt with. As youngsters she was more robust, took the role of beating up anybody who she thought was doing wrong to her brother, kind of protector. As they got a bit older, he neither needed, which he may not have needed in the beginning either, but he neither needed or wanted this, nor was he available to it. Their paths as adults went in quite different directions and her family, when she got divorced, even though her family was not at all religious, they had a strenuous response to her getting divorced, negatively. She saw her husband and her son, particularly her oldest son, much like this twin. She felt that her husband was weak, needed her strength, and therefore wasn't really able to offer her much. She would always have to be in this caretaker role.

Four respondents noted that trauma between siblings, such as molest or abuse, could come up in transference, particularly if the siblings were important in the patient's life. One therapist believed that it may be necessary to work through feelings of shame first when sibling difficulties might manifest, but it is difficult to do so if it is not brought up by the patient. She related a case of a man who had a sexual relationship with his sister as an adult. He can hardly talk about it in the therapy, which the therapist believes is due to shame, although they have worked on it in different ways through boundary issues and intrusiveness in his family that were wounding and hurtful to him.

Sexuality in the sibling relationship

In addition to the example above, when respondents were asked more directly about how sexuality in the sibling relationship might manifest in sibling transference, all but one respondent were able to make statements about how they have experienced this in their work, or might experience it. One therapist is

representative in her thoughts:

> We have few developmental norms for sibling relationships. To fall in love
> with siblings isn't talked about, may be something to explore and talk
> about. It is almost more taboo than any other. If there has been an actual,
> versus a fantasized, sexual relationship, it depends on what the sexual
> relationship was, how it was manifested. If it was abusive, it's going to be
> different than a mutual love affair as a kid. In a sexualized transference,
> they might imagine you were coming on to them. People forget to look at
> siblings with this transference, they look more at mothers and fathers.

The most common example, reported by six of the respondents was that of

having female patients who were sexually abused by older brothers. One female

therapist said that she hasn't seen sibling transference that she's aware of from two

such patients, although they are very unassuming, undemanding, quiet, "really

good girls," who are less likely to have a "squeaky wheel," or angry transference,

with her. They are more likely to withdraw. Another therapist also noted that

women patients who were molested by their brothers may be compliant, "feeling

they have no choice, if they want to stay. They may feel victimized or controlled

if they are angry in the therapy, or they are trying to get rid of me" (#11).

Another therapist noted that transference is complicated in cases of incest

perpetrated by an older brother against a younger sister. She summarized her

experience as follows:

> The transference has less to do with the relationship with the brother, but
> more with the parent's lack or failure to protect, and perception of authority
> figures as pretty useless, coupled with a real anti-authoritarian kind of
> stance. . . . it's very hard, and has led to a failed therapy with one woman.
> She lost out on trust of siblings or of parents. I've not known of this
> between sisters. I've known of it among brothers who have sexual play

between them, mutual sex play without one dominating over the others. (#12)

Two therapists stated that when they are working with patients who have experienced sibling incest, there is less feeling of boundaries with them, and a confusion of love and sex. One therapist spoke of her work with a man who was molested by his older brother for 15 years:

> He's in his 40's, and big and strong, but he's scared of his brother who is out of shape and in his 50's, and I think that he's transferred from there how powerful I might be, how I might hurt him. . . . I think there's been some, not a lot, of sexual transference stuff that has come up, but I wonder, the question comes up, of how it would be when working with a male. He might feel less safe with someone more like his brother who molested him. He might feel more safe because I'm a woman. (#2)

One therapist related the case of a man who seduced his younger sister as a child and felt enormous shame about it in his adult years. This man is close to the age of the therapist, and there was a play in the transference between "his being seductive toward me and his being guilty, or in hiding. . . . it didn't necessarily manifest as guilt per say, shame is a better word" (#10).

A female therapist worked with a woman who felt prematurely forced into sexuality by an older sister's promiscuity and unprotected by her parents. In the transference, her expectation was "I would expect her to be just like me, and would be unable to differentiate my needs from hers . . . and a built in protection that she wanted where she would be protected" (#14).

Another female therapist related the case of a woman who had an older brother she was very close to, and a younger brother she and the older brother treated like a dog, for example, making him crawl around. The older brother had a paternal role and there was a kind of Oedipal relationship with him, but without overt sexuality. He initiated her into many things, especially drugs, which got her into conflict with her parents. This woman had a repetitive dream that a penis could be passed along, sort of like a relay. The penis was detachable, and could be handed over to someone else. The therapist thought that this dream reflected the "initiation business" with the brother, and that it reflected a merger between her and her older brother. The patient and her older brother shared a lot of things. This patient idealized her therapist relentlessly. This therapist believed the patient expected her to stay a bigger person and hold the fort. If she went out of town this patient sometimes got into serious trouble.

A male respondent believed that if sexuality between siblings was traumatic, it could manifest in the transference as mistrust, fear, rage, and difficulty with peers, "so if they see you as a peer, they may distrust you." If the experience was not traumatic and the person finds the therapist attractive, it might manifest as seductiveness, feeling of familiarity, or intimacy. His countertransference is tremendously negative, almost a panic. When this therapist reads about sexual acting out between a patient and a therapist, he imagines that if this happened to him, "I would feel like I had been abandoned by the client as well as vice versa." This therapist was molested by a sibling as a child.

Positive aspects of sibling relationships

When therapists were asked to give examples of positive sibling relationship patterns that might manifest in the transference, all but one were easily able to do so. Their ideas are summarized in Table 6. One respondent said that she doesn't see much positive sibling transference. She has patients who were close to siblings, but there was not "enough stuff to go around in the family, so the good relationship between the siblings was in spite of the family dysfunction, so the positive stuff is harder to feel or maybe is not as noticeable as transference" (#7).

Table 6.

Positive sibling patterns which manifest in transference.

Frequency of response	Respondent #	Positive aspect of sibling relationship seen in transference
5	3, 4, 6, 10, 14	Older sibling as caring, mentor, helpful, empathic.
4	1, 2, 6, 12	Traumatic family, close siblings.
4	2, 13, 15, 16	Countertransference from positive sibling experience.
3	8, 9, 16	Generally, if there is a positive sibling relationship, it gives foundation in transference for sense of love, caring, comfort.
2	5, 13	Experimenting with all kinds of affect with siblings.
1	3	Sibling as best friend, confidant.
1	5	Playfulness, trust.

Five respondents mentioned the idea that patients with older, caring, helpful, or empathic siblings who may have acted as mentors might transfer these feelings onto the therapist. One of these respondents thought that if the patient had a good relationship with an older sibling, he or she may feel that the therapist has knowledge to pass along to them, is not going to humiliate them, that "you have enough goodies, so you will let them have some" (#14). She thought that the patient may sense that the patient and therapist can work toward the common good in a cooperative venture. They can see that the therapist has other patients, but do not feel that this diminishes their relationship. It makes them feel better, "instead of an infantile sense with a sibling that 'of course Mom loves me best of all'." This therapist believed that it takes a certain kind of maturity for a patient to make this realization.

A respondent from a large family thought that children choose an older sibling to be close with, and they work out conflict, competition, and rivalry with the sibling closest to their age. She said that "if I get a patient who is very competitive, I can just sit back and relax because I did all of that with my sister in a lot of different kinds of respects." She described a patient who was a very bright young man, and very competitive. He would come to an interview with two or three typed pages of dreams, or with "this is where we have gone from such and such a period to now." She thought that dealing with this would be very difficult for many therapists, but it was easy for her because of her experience with one of her sisters. She remembered that when she got to be college age, it dawned on her for the first time that she was taller than that sister.

Four respondents spoke of patients from dysfunctional, or abusive, homes where there was intense bonding with siblings. One of these therapists said that such siblings provided a counter reality to the parents which confirmed the patient's experience, and that it would be harder for an only child to trust his or her own judgment vis a vis parent's judgments. Two respondents believed that such trauma bonds can be a salvation, even if the siblings are not close as adults. They may be emotionally isolated from one another as adults, but the trauma bonds are very hard to separate. They said that the positive side of the bonding gave them a strength, sense of safety, and connection that was necessary for survival and that could be transferred to the therapy relationship.

One therapist noticed that in families with role reversals where there has been abuse, the sibling often acted as the parent, and the parent often acted as the sibling. On the positive side, the patient's needs may have been more fulfilled by caretaking siblings which could correlate with better adjustment, and a greater expectation in life and therapy that things will be fair. One respondent said that she is often struck in her work by how little siblings have to do with each other, and that this usually speaks to emotional starvation in the family. She believes that it augers well for the treatment when there is a friendly sibling relationship. She looks at sibling relationships as an indicator of sustained attachment capacity.

Four therapists discussed countertransference resulting from positive aspects of their own sibling relationships. Two stated that they are comfortable with someone who reminds them of their siblings. One therapist found that his close, comfortable relationship with his siblings carried over to expecting this closeness in his own therapy. Another therapist said that he could tell when a patient perceives him as a sibling, and he liked it.

One respondent stated that playfulness and trust could appear in the transference as a result of sibling relationships. He summarized the positive effect of sibling relationships and transference in the following way:

> If someone else has shared the experiences of my life with me, it is possible to do that again in therapy. Siblings can turn to each other, share feelings about others, which can be very positive, a feeling of being seen and known. I think of siblings as being able to tease, play, exercise their power, able to experiment with their feelings, a primary relationship where people can learn to sort of bounce off their own being, experimenting with all kinds of affects early on, such as jealousy, anger, competition, and power. So there is a kind of exploration that can happen as a result of having sibling relationships, one is very prepared for it perhaps (in therapy). (#5)

Topic 3 - The impact and role of authority in regard to sibling transference.

The third topic area, while still looking at factors in the manifestation of sibling transference, asked specifically about the effect of authority in the treatment relationship. The respondents were first asked if they thought that the therapist's authority, as implied in traditional analytic therapy, might interfere with the development or recognition of sibling transference. They were then asked to talk more personally about the role authority plays in their own relationships with patients, and if it has an impact on the development or recognition of sibling transference in their practices.

All of the respondents believed that the role of authority in traditional analytic therapy might interfere with the development or recognition of sibling transference. One therapist provided a good summary of their thoughts in her statement:

> Absolutely, . . . I now use an intersubjective model which talks about and which facilitates looking at any kind of transference. But I think in the traditional psychoanalytical model, it's absolutely set up on the notion that you're a blank screen and they will project their fantasies on you. You're supposed to stay out of the view. But it's set up as a very unequal, authoritative relationship which is so discrepant from what a sibling relationship is, that I think it in many ways could preclude it. (#3)

However, four of the respondents said that if the patient had an authoritative, older, or parentified sibling, sibling transference could be elicited in traditional analysis if the therapist is authoritative or distant. One respondent put it this way:

> I think that there is a hierarchical situation, but it still lends itself nicely to an older-younger sibling transference. In fact it begs for it. So I think that they are pulling for Oedipal rivalry and get it. I actually think that the traditional situation would elicit as much of it as is going to be elicited. (#9)

Five of the respondents believed the traditional analytic approach may not interfere with the development of sibling transference, but could interfere with its recognition. One of the therapists said that the therapist sees what they are willing to look for, and, therefore, if the focus is on the Oedipal constellation, they will see that, or the next layer, the mother-child dyad. Another of these therapists believed the traditional analytic approach could interfere with the recognition of sibling transference because of what she felt was the heavy handedness of some of the traditional analytic points of view; in her opinion, the newer analytic frame is a lot more flexible. She also thought that women tend to do therapy differently from

men in the following way:

> When you look at women who were at the early stages, they still had some
> flexibility and a different way of looking at things. I think women
> generally   tend to teach in a lot of ways because that's their role in the social
> model,   teaching the right way to children and whatever else, so we bring
> that into   therapy, and women pick up on different things. (#13)

When the respondents were asked about the role authority plays with their

own patients, and its impact on sibling transference in their own work, it was

generally more difficult for them to respond to than to previous questions. Ten of

the respondents, the majority, believed that they did have a certain type of

authority and expertise in the treatment relationship. This authority could take

many forms, as one noted:

> It takes a lot of different forms. Sometimes it helps for me to be able to
> pull   rank. People have a certain level of trust in my experience, position, of
> authority. I get projections based on their ideas of my role, my training, my
> title. I think people expect the therapist will be in charge of the boundaries
> around the therapy, when you start and stop, expect to pay you and close
> the door, contain the therapy. In the course of analytic therapy, we break it
> down to see what they are projecting on to me, what they expect from me
> that they expected from other people in authority. It's a major part of the
> work (#5)

One respondent said that many of her patients see her as a kind of

benevolent older sibling, and that there was some countertransference involved in

this because she is the oldest sister in her family. She does not believe that she is a

blank screen, and stated that the spirit of the analyst comes across and is part of

the healing process. She doesn't believe that she actually treats her patients as if they are her younger brother or sister, but "cannot imagine that a fair amount of response is not related to my sibling status" (#9).

Four of the respondents stated they do not make consistent use of authority, but that they were flexible and behaved differently, as needed, with each patient. One noticed that she uses authority differently, depending on whether it is a patient with a personality disorder versus a patient who is neurotic. Another therapist stated that some patients pull for a more familiar, parallel, or equal relationship. Others are really wanting more of an authority, adult, distant figure. Another respondent also thought her use of authority varied. She added that if she is willing to hear herself in the patient's words, "you would discover if the voice of authority is heard from the mother, father, uncle, teacher, or just like my big brother" (#14). Another respondent believed that his background in family systems and object relations laid a foundation for flexibility with authority positions, which would probably make it easier for sibling transference to develop.

Most of the respondents thought that the more authoritarian, or hierarchical, the relationship with the patient was, the more it would pull for a parental transference. The more egalitarian, collegial, or peer-like it was, the more it would pull for sibling transference. However, one therapist stated that it was the other way around, that "if there is going to be sibling transference, they are going to have sibling transference, and they will probably pull for the level of authority that sort of is in line with the kind of transferences that they are likely to have" (#7).

Another therapist who believed that she has authority in the relationship in certain ways, noticed a progression in the transference:

> Yes, I think it does initially (affect development and recognition of sibling transference), and that is why we get so many obviously parental transferences. But it must be correlated with the shift now to allowing us to consider sibling transference, with the shift towards a related type of analytical therapy that has various names, that really accounts more for than two persons in the room. It's a shift away from the so called neutral stance, although I'm actually a strong believer in a certain amount of neutrality. (#10)

Topic 4 - Analytic Dynamics of Sibling Transference

This fourth topic area explored the analytic issues of differentiating parental transference from sibling transference. It also addressed the question of how sibling transference might serve as a resistance to other forms of transference, and how other forms of transference might serve as a resistance to sibling transference.

Differentiation between sibling and parental transference

When asked how they differentiate sibling transference from parental transference, two of the respondents had no response, and one gave a general definition of transference. Three of the respondents said that they really did not know how they would make such a differentiation. All the responses are summarized in Table 7 on the following page.

Common reasons stated for what made it difficult to differentiate parental from sibling transference included: the two overlap; there is no difference in intensity; Oedipal issues are difficult to sort out; and sometimes older siblings take on a parental or caretaking role.

Of the ten therapists who tried to make a differentiation between sibling and parental transference, the most common idea, mentioned by three, was that parental transference has an older, genetic quality, is more embedded, core, or

Table 7.

Means of differentiating sibling and parental transference.

Frequency of response	Respondent #	Means of differentiating transference
3	4, 8, 11	Cannot make a differentiation.
3	2, 3, 12	Difficulty making a differentiation when sibling was in caretaker role.
3	6, 12, 16	Parental transference has old, genetic quality, deeper, more core. Sibling transference is more everyday.
3	7, 9, 13	No response, or gave general definition of transference
2	1, 2	Competition in sibling transference.
2	6, 8	No difference in intensity or strength of parental and sibling transference.
2	5, 12	Problems with authority as parental transference, problems with peers and friends as sibling transference
1	3	Parental transference more influenced by Oedipal issues.
1	5	Difference is evident, feels like sibling rather than parental transference.
1	14	Awareness of different generation between patient and therapist as parental transference, same generation with sibling transference.

deeper for the patient. One therapist expressed it in the following way:

> It overlaps. Parental transference is more core, central, particularly for a small family, only children, first children, or one primarily raised by parents. It's less true with more older siblings, but parental transference still is more central. Siblings are extensions of parents in the child's mind and are transmitting agents of parental love, concern, and resentments. It can be experienced as a loss of self for the older sibling, carrying the parent's feelings and attitudes. (#16)

Along these lines, one therapist believed parental transference is more influenced by Oedipal issues. Another said that one has an "awareness of different generations with parental transference versus (with sibling transference) there is a sense of the two of us in a same generational relationship" (R. #14).

Two of the respondents thought that one of the key differences between the parental and sibling relationships and transference was authority. However, they felt that this can get blurred when there is an older sibling taking on a parental role, or a parent abdicating responsibility to a sibling. One of these therapists said that sometimes the difference between sibling and parental transference feels evident to her. She gave the example of a man coming in who had problems with his boss, authority problems, and who presented more parental transference in his relationship with her. When this man talks about a problem with a friend, she sees it may be more sibling transference. She thinks that transference is fluid, depending on the focus and transference shifts, and that it was helpful to be aware of the shifts and pulls in the transference.

Competition stood out for two therapists as the means to differentiate parental and sibling transference. Two of the respondents believe that knowledge of the patient and his or her family background would enable them to make such a differentiation.

<u>Resistance</u>

<u>Sibling transference as a resistance to other forms of transference</u>. When asked if they had experienced a sibling transference that seemed to serve as a resistance to other forms of transference, eight of the respondents said that they had not, or may have, but were not aware of it. One of these six therapists was representative of this group in her feeling that it is more likely that the emphasis on the parent child relationship would allow both the therapist and patient to collude in resistance to sibling transference. She thought that in classical psychoanalytic theory transference is essentially defined as the Oedipal relationship. When a therapist takes someone into therapy, no matter what the viewpoint, she felt that the therapist identifies with the patient as an injured child, which makes it hard to identify the patient as a parent or a sibling.

The respondents who believed they had experienced such resistance had different experiences. One male therapist said that sibling issues and transference are embedded in the parental relationship, and vice versa. One female therapist thought that she had experienced patients whose sibling transference was a resistance to a sexualized or erotic transference. She thought that sibling transference could also be a resistance to maternal or paternal transference. She gave the example of a male patient who was about her age. He was training to be a psychologist, and he wanted to be taken care of, but any time he would feel threatened, he would move to see her more like a sister.

Another female therapist thought of a woman patient who had been molested by her father and brother. She focused on her brother because it was too hard to focus on her father. This therapist believed that such resistance in the transference could happen with a "good/bad split when the parent gets to be the bad person, and the sibling gets to be the good person, or vice versa" (#11).

One therapist gave the example of a patient who said about the treatment, "this isn't what I expected, it seems more like a friendship developing" (#5). The therapist thought this could be helpful, and imply maternal giving and sharing, or maybe feelings of disappointment, but he also believed that such feeling could serve as a distraction from other feelings or transferences.

Another therapist worked with a woman who had a younger sister who was very dependent, clingy, and fragile. This interfered with her ability to attach, become more dependent in therapy, and develop transference with the therapist. It repelled her and felt dangerous to see or experience her the way she did her sister, and "so it is hard for her to develop the kind of transference onto me that she needs to, the kind of parental transference" (#7).

Another case illustrating difficulties with a sister was related by a female respondent. A patient of hers has problems with the way she looks, and feels that the therapist cannot understand her problems whatsoever. This therapist believes that the patient experiences her as her sister who is thin and pretty. It is easier for her to get involved in her envy of the therapist, as she envied her sister, than to deal with her mother's message, who wasn't as concerned with looks and dress.

Another therapist related the case of a patient who she believed had a positive kind of twinship sibling transference with her that could be a defense against other more critical or disappointed feelings.

Other forms of transference as resistance to sibling transference.
Respondents were next asked if they had experienced cases in which some form of transference served as a resistance to sibling transference. Seven of them were not aware of having experienced this. One of these respondents said that she could not think of such a case because she does not see transferences as discrete. She thought that if there are two transferences operating, there is so much overlap that it could not be sorted out in this way.

Two therapists thought this occurred, but could not think of a specific case example. Although another therapist thought of one case where this occurred, she expressed her experience in this way:

> You don't get to the sibling transference until you've worked through the other, but I think there is a form of transference, namely first love of life after family, the first real relationship, generally in mid to late adolescence, early 20's. A lot of stuff gets formed at that point developmentally, and that person can have an enormous influence on the person's life, even if it doesn't last long, but if it's meaningful. I would imagine that would also rival the siblings, may be stronger   in some cases where there was a
fairly   benign relationship among siblings. (#10)

Again, those therapists who had experienced some other form of transference as resistance to sibling transference, gave very different examples.

One therapist gave a more general response, saying that he could think of cases where the patient had a hard time exploring the depths of their feelings about siblings. These feelings were painful and troubling to them, and "hard work to do" (#5). Siblings are extremely important to them, and this respondent thought that therapists have focused more on the absent or abusive parent or depressed mother instead. He talked about the importance of siblings in large families, and the sense of connectedness that comes from reconnecting with siblings later in life.

Another therapist said that she had experienced other transference as a resistance to sibling transference. She added that this often feels like peeling layers, and can be frightening to have in the room when it's a loaded or difficult relationship with a sibling. One therapist said that when sibling transference is sexualized and the parental transference is safer, patients prefer to focus on that. He gave the example of a woman who had a sexualized, abusive relationship with her older brother. He was harder to deal with than her mother, at whom she was angry, "but it was a safe anger" (#16). Her relationship with her mother wasn't comfortable, but it was stable in a certain way, whereas the sibling relationship was much more volatile and problematic. She loved her brother and depended on him, and he sexualized it, so she felt deeply betrayed. She depended on him because the mother was perfectionistic and rejecting.

One respondent saw a man for 14 months in analysis before he mentioned that he had a brother living in the same city, only ten minutes away. Although she expressed concern that her own experience of her several siblings might bias her, she also believed that it was important that her patient didn't mention this sibling. She thought that this might be due to some form of sibling transference.

Lastly, a respondent described a case of a female patient with a sister who was born when she was 10 years old. This birth reunited her divorced parents. The patient could only talk about loving and adoring her sister, but "she had horrible problems of jealousy, feeling slighted, everything you would associate with sibling transference, and she would get so angry with me, presumptuous, intrusive, and critical of me. She couldn't face some of the darker feelings she had about her sister " (#7). This case example seemed to illustrate the role of resistance to sibling transference.

Topic 5 - Psychoanalytic Theory and Training Regarding Sibling Transference

In this next focus of inquiry, therapists were asked about their beliefs regarding whether or not a theoretical gap exists in relation to sibling transference, and, if there is such a gap, what might account for it. They described professional training they had received on sibling transference, assessed its importance in treatment, and how awareness of it might affect treatment.

Theoretical gap regarding sibling transference

All of the respondents thought that there was a theoretical gap regarding sibling transference and that the topic was underrepresented in literature. Two respondents mentioned Kohut's idea of twinship transference as the only theory which approximated a theory of sibling transference. Another respondent said that she has noticed little written about siblings or friends, which seemed related to her.

In her 19 years of experience she had only seen a handful of related articles,

including some by George Polluck on sibling loss. It seemed interesting to her

that he did work on siblings, and is now doing a book on friends. Several of the

respondents said that the only book they had read related to siblings was The

Sibling Bond (1982) by Bank and Kahn.

The possible reasons given by the respondents for such a gap are

summarized in Table 8. A therapist who has been practicing over 15 years, both

in the United States and Britain, made the following statement which summarizes

the most prevalent idea:

> You mean the missing hunks of literature on the matter. Yes. Absolutely.
> Only in recent years have we noticed how important siblings are, and that
> may come out of the change to a more interpersonal type therapy. People
> have been dismissive, which is surprising when you think about Anna
> Freud's work with children who came out of the camps. She noticed how
> surprisingly healthy they were, that they had parented each other, and had
> been their significant constant objects. I think we've all heard of the only
> child syndrome. When you're in therapy with someone who is an only
> child, it does have a different quality. They are much more entitled to all of
> what they get. So part of the gap is due to the focus on parents. Even with
> Anna Freud's work, we were all so surprised. I do think it's focused
> partially on parents because of the enormous authority imbibed in
> themselves, particularly as analysts, where the majority of work in Britain,
> where theoretical work comes from. (#10)

Table 8.

Possible reasons for the existence of a theoretical gap regarding sibling

transference.

Frequency of response	Respondent #	Reason for theoretical gap.
6	1, 3, 6, 8, 10, 15	Focus on parents in general, not on siblings
6	3, 4, 7, 12, 13, 15	Emphasis of Freudian psychoanalytic theory on parents.
3	12, 13, 16	Freudian theory from a Caucasian, European culture with emphasis on individualism.
2	2, 11	No reason given.
2	4, 15	Something powerful about what siblings mean to each other that makes it difficult to look at, i.e. sexuality issues.
2	3, 5	Developmental theories focus on parents.
2	10, 16	Focus on parents because of authority investment as analysts.
2	13, 14	Looked at how siblings relate to parents, not each other, focus on parent-child dyad.
1	9	Sibling seen as satellite to core representation with parent.
1	9	Sibling thought about only in real terms.
1	14	Therapist own narcissism.

Five other respondents believed that a theoretical gap existed regarding sibling

transference due to a primary focus on parents in treatment and transference.

The second most prevalent idea given is that the gap is due to a larger

problem of psychoanalytic theory not looking at sibling issues in general, not just

sibling transference. One therapist summarized it this way:

> There's a lot of short shrift given to the actual quality of the relationship
> with siblings, how they develop and shape a person, which is obviously

related to the transference issue. The effect of development has been heavily influenced by Freudian theory, with the emphasis on mothers and fathers, and siblings just kind of come along, or get in the way, or cause you to lose your parents' attention, and the complexity of those relationships are not considered in terms of how they lead into development. Therefore, the same gap holds for sibling transference. It also had to do with a very conservative notion of transference, for example, if the definition of transference is historical, you have ghosts in the nursery which is very historical, parents, either real or imagined, and then you regress in the work. You're going to have a gap in terms of the family. If you talk about different kinds of transference from a more developmental model, then the gap is due to the larger gap of lack of attention to the family. (#3)

Another therapist also thought that developmental psychoanalytic theory was developed by a narrow, dyadic model, primarily involved with mothers and their children. He thought that theory has expanded recently to include more systems ideas in psychoanalytic thought, for example, issues around triangulation and research he did on the role and experience of the father. He thought the primarily parent-child focus was now shifting to include other caretakers, but is very slow to develop because the mother-child, parent-child relationship is so primary. He pointed out that family systems practitioners and theorists have looked at life cycle issues, such as a child displaced by the birth of a sibling.

One African/American therapist said that she has been interested in siblings and transference because she came from a family of nine siblings, but she has found little written about it in her 36 years of practice, other than The Sibling Bond (1982). She thought that when therapists first started developing a theoretical frame of reference, they looked at it from a broad perspective of how do siblings relate to their parents, and not how do siblings relate to each other, and what this means. She pointed out that we've paid attention to the bond of mother to child, but haven't looked at how siblings bond, how a younger sister might bond to an older sister rather than a mother. She remembered Jane Goodall's studies of baboons in which older siblings were observed giving love and support until the mother came in and took authority. This African/American respondent also pointed out that psychoanalysis grew up in Europe, "and that's patriarchal, so that would have some semblance of where the gap comes from and why it hasn't been developed more" (#13).

Another African/American respondent repeated this idea in his statement that a theoretical gap regarding sibling transference existed due to the trajectory of the development of psychotherapy:

> It came out of authoritarian models; Freud, Jung, male, medical, traditional society, and people in high positions. It tended to elicit parental transference, tuned into it. It was not tuned into egalitarian aspects of the relationship. It overlooked other forms of transference, and we have built on the parental transference model. I see countertransference, in some ways, as far more significant, but there is less focus on how it is dealt with. Transference is a more authoritarian issue. Traditional analysis uses a cultural model involving power over others, so they don't look inside at countertransference or more egalitarian transferences because they are not seen as empowering. (#16)

Another therapist echoed this theme in her idea that psychology in the United States came from roots in Freud in Germany, and white, European culture, with an emphasis on individualism, in contrast to other cultures where families and groups are more important, and this has created a theoretical gap regarding sibling transference.

Two therapists thought the gap could be due to resistance "because it can bring up a lot, for example, the sexuality issues we talked about, particularly with cross gender sibs" (#15). The second therapist thought that the influence of Freud explained the beginning of why a gap was present, but not that there is almost nothing in the literature at the present time. It seemed to her that there must be something rather powerful about sibling relationships, something about what siblings mean to each other, that has made it difficult to look at.

One therapist had a different way of looking at the theoretical gap regarding sibling transference. When asked what might cause such a gap, she said:

> Our own narcissism, for example, when I was pregnant, I noticed there was a literature and interest in the effect of the therapist's pregnancy on the patient, but found there was nothing in the literature about the therapist's response to the patient's pregnancy. There is a way we want to focus on the dyadic relationship of either the parent or the child and don't want to let the sibling in, to look at sibling transference. Sibling transference is almost always dyadic. (#14)

Training

When asked if they had received information regarding sibling transference or countertransference in their professional training, eight respondents said they had never received any such training. Three respondents said they had only received information through readings on their own.

One respondent said that she originally received no information in her training on sibling transference, but subsequently has through both case consultation and her involvement in a reading seminar where it is a major topic. Another respondent remembered reading <u>The Sibling Bond</u> (1982) in graduate school. He was interested in family life cycle development, but felt he was not trained in it as a transference issue. Most of his training regarding sibling transference came from consultation. Another therapist also did not receive any formal training on sibling transference, but did read about sibling configuration and issues for his own thesis.

One therapist said that she had a degree in Family Psychology, and sibling transference was never talked about in the training. She is in year two of a three year program at the Masterson's Institute, which she feels is psychoanalytic, and it has not been discussed. She thought that it got passed over for parental transference, perhaps because it is so overlapping and difficult to sort out.

Importance of sibling transference

The majority of the respondents, thirteen, believed that sibling transference is an important aspect of treatment. One respondent did not able to address the question due to time limits. The positive feelings regarding its importance included ideas such as: intimacy, closeness, and attachment with siblings as powerful issues and contributing to transference with one's children as well; that the dynamics of siblings in large families are an important aspect in treatment; that it will become even more important in the future with the focus on blended families, step-relatives, and siblings.

Two respondents were more equivocal regarding the importance of sibling transference. One said that sometimes it is important and sometimes it is not, and that it is good to work with it when it's there. Another said it was important, but not really in the way she conceptualized transference. She believed it was important only in the sense that siblings are objects which are important to be considered in their representation.

Effect of awareness of sibling transference on treatment

Respondents were next asked how they thought awareness of sibling transference and countertransference might effect treatment. One respondent did not address this question due to time limitations, but all the other respondents talked positively about the contribution of working with sibling transference. Several said it would enrich the treatment. One therapist exemplified this feeling in his thought that sibling transference occurs, and the more one attends to it, the richer the therapy experience is going to be. He said it would broaden one's scope of interpretation, and that the more awareness we can have, the more we can be effective. Another therapist thought treatment would be deeper and more complete if one works with sibling transference, and that it might make treatment last longer.

One therapist also thought that working with sibling transference would deepen treatment because it would bring up more texture that's being missed. He thought that one way it could contribute to treatment is in the direction of a more equalized relationship between patient and therapist, where the therapist is not just an authority, but sometimes a sibling, and sometimes a younger sibling appearing unequal. Generally, he believed that it "underlies peer aspects in therapy" (#16).

Six of the respondents spoke of the importance of siblings or lack of siblings in terms of self development, later relationships with peers and partners, and in work settings. They believed that working with sibling transference would enhance growth and closeness with others in all these areas. The following is a good example of this group:

> I do think that our notions of what relationships are like, what we ourselves are like, and what male/female relationships are like, are very much influenced by our relationships with our siblings, and what we really see in that intimacy of the family setting, and being together on family vacations, and together when parents go out, and that kind of enforced intimacy for all those early years, and I think that there are . . . so many different kinds of feelings and ideas that get transmitted among siblings that parents aren't privy to, and they really do have their own relationship and their own kind of way of understanding each other, and I do think that tremendously affects choices that we make; what you look for in a mate, what you look for in a relationship, the way you see yourself in the world. So I think that it is a whole area that deserves a lot more attention. I think it could be very enriching to look into the whole aspect of sibling transference opposed to much more focusing on the parental transference. (#6)

Another therapist agreed that working with sibling transference is important in terms of how we relate to friends, partners, and issues of envy. She thought it comes up with achievement and some losses, especially when doing something in the outside professional community with those patients who are also in the field.

Topic 6 - Respondent birth order and sense of sibling transference issues

The birth order of the respondents is summarized in Table 1. Again, there was variation in birth order. One respondent was an only child, and one was a female of a male/female twin pair with one older brother. Seven were first-born of multiple sibling groups, ranging from one to six siblings. Six respondents were second born of either one or two siblings. Three were the youngest of multiple sibling groups of three, six, and nine.

As noted, several respondents discussed personal issues with siblings, sibling transference and countertransference in their earlier responses. However, when asked more specifically what was their sense of their own transference issues in regard to siblings, all respondents were able to give further information regarding their feelings and experiences.

The respondent who was an only child said that she may not see sibling transference if it is there, recognize it, or give it the importance it deserves, given her status as an only child. The respondent who has a twin brother and an older brother said that she was more competitive with her older brother, and closer to her twin brother. Even though they were all competitive, they each would definitely stick up for one another, even if this meant not revealing to her parents who did something. When asked how this might appear in terms of transference issues, she was not sure and stated that she would need more time to think about it.

The major theme mentioned by respondents who were first-born was the effect of being in a position of responsibility and caretaking for younger siblings. The first-born from the largest sibling group of six children stated that she paved the way for her siblings, acting as the big sister. She did not believe there was gender bias in her family, so she didn't have the impact of "oh, how unfortunate that the oldest is a girl." Because she has a lot of siblings, she thought it was conceivable that unconsciously, "in a countertransferential way, I might behave towards some patients in a way that is kind of big sister like" (#9).

The therapist who is the first of four boys in his family said that he tended to be more of the caretaker in his family as the oldest, more parentified child. He thought his work as a therapist, "which includes taking care of people, and orchestrating things around their needs, fits very well with my own issues" (#5). He believed that he had gone through enough therapy to understand this, and the feelings of resentment which he had, and responsibility issues in his life. He thought these issues came up in various ways, both with some of the positive traits and some that could get him in trouble.

Another first-born (#4), had a younger brother. She said that she was the good, responsible child who took care of her parents. Her brother was the acting out child who had all the freedom and got away with not attending to family things. She believes this can appear in countertransference as a greater vulnerability to taking her own experience and assuming it might be like the patient's experience. She might interpret from her own experience, rather than listening or hearing what had actually happened to the person, which might not be the same. She sees her perceptions of dyads, larger family groups, or single parents as a potentially significant issue. She always wanted to be a part of a larger family, and feels she may not see some of the disadvantages of being taken care of by others.

Another first-born also talked about the caretaking role she had in her family. She was the oldest of three sisters, and had intense, close, powerful relationships with them. She was a mother figure for both sisters. She said that "growing up they were like flies on the wall to me, annoyances, but since I was out of the house, and they were also married and were in their own lives, I became . . . very involved, and a strong mother figure, a real kind of caretaking figure, which is very much sort of my role in general in the world, so it carries through in those relationships" (#6).

One therapist was the first-born of three children, with a younger sister and brother. She said that early in her training she had a couple in therapy who were younger siblings, and she didn't know what they were talking about. She believed she was profoundly affected by being the parent of two children. It enabled her to identify with the experience of both her youngest and oldest child. If she only had one child, she believed that she probably would still not understand the experience of the youngest, although some understanding simply comes from maturity for her. She thought something which is not talked about or understood is what it means to assimilate that parents can see their child's limitations but that doesn't diminish their love for the child, but from the child's perspective it does. The child feels they should be loved first and best of all. Maturity is coming to the position of understanding that parent's don't love children for good or bad qualities. This respondent believed that this "is where the struggle is, accepting the unconditional love of the parent and that that means unconditionally loving the sibling as well" (#14).

There were three middle children in the study, each with different experiences with siblings and transference. One (#3) was the second of three children, with two brothers. She said that she has been a younger sister and a second maternal figure for her younger brother, so she has different transference associations. She was very close to her older brother who was protective towards her. She experienced some gender difference with this brother. She didn't want to think that there were things he could do that she could not, so she looked up to him and tried to keep up with him. She thought that the way this comes up in transference is that if she feels someone is treating her like a younger sister, putting her down, she can "get her back up." In general, she felt her transference with her brothers, as a feminist in relation to men, is that she loves them very much, and she competes with them. In terms of her younger brother who she helped raise and enjoyed, she feels that he was the first of her children. She has two children of her own, and feels that she has "plenty of sibling/maternal feelings that come up in my practice."

Another middle child (#7), is the second of three girls. She said that her oldest sister is self centered, and knows everything. This "drives me crazy, so I can't stand people who know everything, it infuriates me, so I feel protective in certain relationships of what I know." She believed that she didn't have as much transference, or "stuff" with her younger sister, although this sister can evoke her wanting to be the one who can do everything for her, and she sometimes gets carried away with this. She said that there wasn't enough to go around in her family, so she is jealous and sensitive about being left out.

The last middle respondent who was a middle child (#10) is the second of three with an older brother and a younger sister. She spoke of countertransference she had in relation to both siblings. They were only 18 months apart and had intense relationships with one another. She and her older brother were like twins. They were raised in England and he was sent to boarding school when he was eight and she was seven. This set up a kind of romantic loss and longing for him. Once in a while she experiences this with particular male patients.

She said that her more difficult experience is with her younger sister, "who maintains that I was a bully, and I experienced her as withholding, so if I am with someone very near to my age who is being withholding, it will bring up my mean big sister thing." In her own therapies, none of her therapist dealt with her sibling issues. She was in therapy with a man who was sexually inappropriate in a verbal way with her. She did not like him, but part of her got the similar kinds of feelings she had with her brother at times. This man was closer in age to her than "sort of a father figure, I hadn't gotten in touch with those kinds of longings for my father at that particular juncture in my life."

Three respondents were the second of two children. One of these respondents has a brother who is three and one-half years older. She said she was brought up by her brother. He did things like going to the school nurse to see how much sleep she should be getting when he thought she wasn't getting enough sleep in elementary school. She thought that it was hard for her to differentiate brother from paternal transference. Her therapist will sometimes say the transference "as being with my Dad, it's really that I'm seeing him as brother, because Dad was pretty absent" (# 2). If her therapist misses a session, it feels like her Dad who wasn't there for her. But a lot of times she feels the transference is about her brother and not her father. Competition is another way she experiences transference related to her brother. She also thought that her brother was a child raising a child, and he was unable to come through in many ways for her, so this comes up in a negative transference with her therapist.

Another respondent (#8) who also was the second child with an older brother, said that her relationship with her father and brother overlapped. She said that they were so absent from her life, and from her internal life, that she can have low expectations of men. These low expectations interlock for her with cultural expectations, "a gender difference, below expectation of men's relationship to relationships." For a long time, when a man started crying she was taken a back, and this had an impact on her as a therapist in her early years. She still has to watch levels of this where she has less expectations of men, such as couples therapy.

Another therapist (#1) was also the second child with an older brother. She thought that her feelings and possible transferences related to her brother were not well formed because he was much older than her, and seemed like an uncle. He was killed in the service overseas as a young man, so she has few memories of him other than idealization. Sometimes he would get her things that her parent's could not afford, so he was like an adult figure that provided for her. She felt that "it's a very kind of missing pieces kind of sibling story."

Three respondents were the youngest of larger sibling groups. One (#15) was the third child of three, with two older sisters. He thought that he had usurped his sister's position as the youngest and male, and this made him feel guilt sometimes. He also thought that he made himself invisible at times because of this position. His father was closest to his middle sister who acted out more, and his mother was closest to him. When he was younger he often found himself in the role of mediating between his middle sister and his mother. He thought this might have influenced his choice to become a therapist. As he got older, he sometimes just wanted his middle sister to leave when she was acting out, and fantasized what the family would be like without her. He thought that this comes up as countertransference with patients who are difficult in his desire for them to leave. He has also noticed this in his supervision of interns, and thought that it might be related to their own sibling issues. Overall, he feels that he is able to make new friends more easily with women because of his experience with his sisters.

Another therapist (#16) is the youngest of six children. He has three sisters and two brothers. He was sexually abused by an older brother and believed that this was "the main piece that was problematic." He said that he was so aware of this that it doesn't come up too much without his seeing it. Sometimes he feels betrayed by patients who are narcissistic. He described a male patient who was annoying, and whenever he tried to help him, it made the patient angry. This respondent also said that he has a strong negative reaction when he reads about a therapist sexually abusing patients. Generally he said that when he likes a patient, part of where he is coming from is that they remind him of a sibling, or he feels the way he felt with a sibling.

The respondent from the largest family (#13) was from a sibling group of nine. She was the youngest with four older brothers and four older sisters. She said that her family spanned three generations in two. Her oldest siblings were old enough to be her parents, so she thought some of her transference with them is "trying to look at authority from a traditional sense, as well as to look at it from a sense of where I came from in terms of questioning authority a great deal." They were her sibling, so she felt she could question them in that way, and "so, if they were my siblings, then that's how I view the world."

The very last question asked respondents if there was anything that had not covered that was pertinent that they wanted to add. Only two of the respondents added further information. One respondent repeated her stance from a "post modern perspective" in the following way:

> I think there are certain concepts that we privilege, hold dear, that we overdo in our field. One of them is the privileging of early childhood material, that early childhood issues have a deeper impact on someone than

deciding to become a parent. I also don't privilege the transference, as that if you work in vivo with the transference it's going to be better work than if we work the client issues to everyone else, including the siblings. Where the transference, where it hums along, this isn't the projected transference, but that there is a safety in the relationships so that the client can really look at his or her relationship to the sibling in a more intrapsychic way. I don't hold transference as the most important element in psychotherapy, I actually think that transference is a narrative, so that's why I have trouble with these questions. I work it when it feels present, and I don't pull for it very much. (#8)

Another therapist repeated her thought that sibling transference will

manifest differently, depending on the limit of the patient's disturbance. She

stated that she was interested in how sibling transference effects relationships with

co-workers, and what doesn't happen with only children. She thought it would be

interesting to do a study comparing families with siblings versus only children.

Summary

The major findings of this study were:

1. Therapists were excited to discuss this topic and talked about a few aspects of

   it clearly, such as sexuality in sibling transference and the effect of their own

   birth order on countertransference. However, they generally found it difficult

   to articulate thoughts, beliefs, and experiences on the topic when questioned.

2. Few of the respondents received training of any form regarding sibling

   transference.

3. Sibling transference manifested most commonly in the treatment relationship

   in the form of competition and envy. Other common forms that difficulties in sibling relationships took in the treatment relationship were abuse, caretaking, or parentification.

4. Many different factors elicited sibling transference, such as age, race, gender, and the demeanor of the therapist, or events in the life of the patient or therapist.

5. Countertransference responses related to siblings were reported by all of the respondents.

6. The role of authority in traditional analytic therapy interfered with the development or recognition of sibling transference, unless the patient had an older, authoritative sibling.

Respondents believed there is a theoretical gap regarding sibling transference due to a focus on parents in general, rather than siblings in theory and literature, and an emphasis in Freudian, psychoanalytic theory on parents, as well as its genesis in a Caucasian, European culture which values individualism.

CHAPTER 4

Discussion

This chapter addresses the following topics: interpretation of results, limitations of this study, and implications for future research. Implications for clinical practice and training will be included in the interpretation of results.

Interpretation of the Results

All of the respondents in this study reported the same experience noted by the limited number of authors who have addressed the topic of sibling transference, namely, that they have encountered little discussion of sibling transference in literature, theory, or training. This study was designed to contribute to this paucity of information by gathering feedback from a small sample of experienced therapists regarding how sibling transference might manifest in their clinical practice, training, and theoretical framework. The respondents in this study were almost all excited and eager to begin some form of a dialogue in a topic area which they felt was relatively unexplored.

The main findings of this study support the ideas expressed in the literature. For example, the finding that few of the respondents had received any training or information on this topic supports the contention of the literature that sibling transference is a neglected subject.

Several respondents had read the book, The Sibling Bond (Bank and Kahn, 1982), showing that these therapists were interested in the topic and willing to learn more about it on their own. Implications for training will be discussed in a later section of this chapter.

Theory

Most respondents agreed with the finding in the literature that there exists a theoretical gap regarding sibling transference, and the reasons why such a gap exists. The idea that Freudian theory, with its focus on parents in the transference experience, has resulted in the neglect of the role of siblings, was stated by many therapists in this study and most of the literature, with the exception of Lasky and Mulliken (1988) and Colonna and Newman (1983). Respondents also mentioned the role of culture in this context, noticing that Freudian theory evolved in a primarily European, Caucasian culture which emphasizes individualism. This emphasis on the individual may have led to a theory that failed to take into consideration the importance of and contributions made by other family members, including extended family groups.

Only one respondent spoke to Ian Graham's (1988) idea that the lack of attention to sibling issues may be due to a contempt of familiarity. He thought that the imminence of personal, familial, organizational, and clinical associations to the topic make it difficult to reflect on with sufficient detachment. Respondents did not mention this factor which may be due to the very same phenomenon, namely, that they lacked sufficient detachment to be aware of this factor.

The literature also mentioned that both developmental and analytic theory in general have focused on the role and importance of parents, leaving out siblings as important objects, and this focus is reflected in the theory of transference as well. Several respondents agreed with this. They expressed the hope, however, that newer analytic and developmental models would have a more collaborative and multi-dimensional approach to the therapeutic relationship, allowing for the importance of others besides parents in the patient's life. Most respondents believed that newer approaches which considered the role of mutual influence in the therapy dyad also were more open to a more differentiated, complex model with a sense of fluidity, change, and interrelated internal and external object relationships.

Conversely, again in line with the literature, many of the respondents were of the opinion that more authoritarian, traditional analytic approaches interfere with the development or recognition of sibling transference, unless the sibling was older and authoritarian.

Ruth Lesser (1978) summarized this in her statement that the analyst cannot limit him or herself to a single role, but "must allow her/himself to be transformed into a sibling as well as a parent" (p. 48).

Factors and Analytic Dynamics

Although most therapists were able to name one or two factors which they felt contributed to sibling transference, it was difficult for them to do so, and they frequently asked the interviewer what was in the literature and research. They also had difficulty thinking about such applied questions as how they used their authority as therapists and the impact of that on the development of sibling transference, how they differentiated between parental and sibling transference, and whether they had observed cases in which sibling transference might have acted as a resistance to other transferences and vice versa.

Only two respondents attempted to address the question of differentiation between Oedipal sibling and parental triangles, as discussed by Sharpe and Rosenblatt (1994), and they were unclear in their answers. This difficulty formulating, retrieving, synthesizing, and describing sibling transference experiences may have been primarily due to the fact that this topic was new for most respondents, or as mentioned earlier, that they experienced difficulty getting sufficient detachment.

From another perspective, Cesio (1993) noted that Freud stressed that it is relatively easy to interpret the patient's material, "that is, the transferences to the preconscious representations, particularly free associations" (p. 131), but that there was difficulty inherent in handling the patient's transference to the analyst. As Freud expressed it:

> This (transference to the person of the physician) happens . . . to be by far the hardest part of the whole task. It is easy to learn how to interpret dreams, to extract from the patient's associations his unconscious thoughts and memories, and to practice similar explanatory arts: for these the patient himself will always provide the text. Transference (to the person of the physician) is the one thing the presence of which has to be detected almost without assistance and with only the slightest clues to go upon. (1905e/1953)

Given this difficulty in handling transference to the analyst, in general, and the dearth of knowledge about sibling transference in particular, it is not surprising that respondents had difficulty conceptualizing and articulating their experience with regard to this issue.

This difficulty could also be related to the analyst's preconscious recently described by Victoria Hamilton (1996), with the hypothesis that awareness of sibling transference for many therapists resides in this preconscious area. This preconscious area lies between more deeply unconscious (private) beliefs and conscious (public) declarations.

Freud discussed the preconscious and it was later elaborated by Balint (1957) and Winnicott (1953) as the "third" or "intermediate" area of the mind. This preconscious area is hard to articulate and is not easily represented in the languages of either the primary or secondary processes, according to Hamilton. The preconscious consists of various descriptions of the maps or sketches analysts draw of the routes they follow in their daily practice. Hamilton conducted a study from 1988 to 1990 in which she interviewed analysts in America and Britain through a similar questionnaire method. She examined what analysts say about what they think and do to flesh out what she termed the protected, largely theoretical debate on the ways beliefs relate to one another and are enacted in clinical practice. The analysts in the study were asked to describe their use of specific concepts, such as transference and real relationship. She found that even when they were familiar with the particular topic under discussion, may have even taught what it was supposed to mean, "they found it hard to gather up the scattered uses of that concept throughout their current practice" (p. 6).

Hamilton noted that Wittgenstein (cited in Budd, 1993) pointed out that, although we are trained or encouraged to master the use of words, we are not taught to describe that use. Wittgenstein gave many examples of how "the possession of one ability does not guarantee the possession of a related, higher-level ability" (p. 5). Hamilton summarizes this in relation to her study in the following way:

> Wittgenstein offered the examples of how we might imagine that we could find our way around a city extremely well and easily take the shortest route from one place to another, and yet we could not draw a map of that city. And when we do try to draw a map, we go completely wrong. Thus, the maps or theoretical models that analysts construct of the ways they use specific concepts can be misleading. (p. 5)

Again, in this study, the difficulty respondents had describing and explaining their experiences with sibling transference was very apparent, although most were very excited about the potential space to do so. One area where they were consistently more able to recall and describe case examples was with reference to questions about sexuality in the sibling relationship and its manifestation in the transference. This might be due to the attention that has been given to treating sexual abuse and erotic transference in recent years, since most of the case examples described some form of sexual abuse by siblings. It could also be due to anxieties regarding erotic transferences and ensuing attention paid to these experiences.

It is interesting to note that two of the three male respondents were fathers and had done research of some form on their own on the impact of fathers on the family and sibling issues. It seems that their experience as contributing to and interrupting the mother-child dyad in their families created a space to emotionally appreciate the role of another family member in object relations and development. Muir (1989) points out the role of both fathers and siblings in development of attachment:

> It has become clear that the father, or for that matter an older sibling, may become (or be from the beginning) the primary attachment figure for the child. Does this answer the question, Can the father be an object in the psychoanalytic sense? Of course, the answer has always been yes, an exciting oedipal object, for example-in line with the libido theory. However, attachment theory takes us further by positing a hierarchy of attachment figures that can, in preferential order, insulate the infant against the experience of aloneness, strangeness, and danger. (p. 49)

The two fathers in this study were able to talk with interest and ease about their personal and transference experiences with sibling issues. Again, this may be due to the opening they experienced in the potential space of object relations as fathers.

Just as these fathers were able to discuss sibling transference with relative ease, it was also interesting to note that both African/American therapists easily articulated their beliefs about why a theoretical gap may exist regarding sibling transference, noting the role of cultural bias. Again, due to the very small number of respondents, one could not draw any conclusions, but the experience of these two respondents supports an interesting hypothesis that being placed in the role of the other, particularly in a minority role, may lend itself to greater awareness of the impact of others in the development of, and resistance to, such awareness due to issues of power.

In terms of other findings, the fact that the most commonly mentioned experience of sibling issues in the transference were competition and envy, may have been influenced by the attention paid to these real object relationship issues between siblings. It could also be due to the primacy of these feelings for the respondents in their own sibling relationships.

Lesser (1978) believes that Freud may have effected a disproportionate emphasis on competitive strivings among siblings in his statement that "children are completely egoistic; they feel their needs intensely and strive ruthlessly to satisfy them-especially as against the rivals, other children, and first and foremost as against their brothers and sisters" (Freud, 1900/1953, p. 250). Lesser believes that this has led to attention to competition rather than positive interactions with siblings. She points out that affectionate attitudes have traditionally been viewed as a cover for more basic rivalry for parental love, common possessions, and living space (1978). Perhaps respondents in this study were influenced by these aspects of Freudian theory.

It was surprising that sibling loss was mentioned by very few respondents as a factor impacting the development of sibling transference, given the importance attributed to it in the literature. Perhaps there is some resistance to acknowledging the impact of sibling loss. Denial may serve as a means to cope with the intensity of the loss or identification with the lost sibling which would make articulating the experience difficult. Another possibility would be denial or repression used as a defense against wishes for parricide and ensuing guilt, making discussion of sibling loss difficult. This is simply conjecture, and another possibility is that many of the respondents may not have experienced sibling loss, making it less apparent as a factor in sibling transference.

Birth Order

Bank and Kahn (1982) state that many therapists are first-born and may have experienced dispossession of maternal attention by later-born siblings, contributing to less therapeutic tolerance for younger siblings or for building sibling bonds in therapy. First-born therapists were the largest group, a total seven respondents, in this sample. Two of the first-borns did discuss having little tolerance for younger siblings, but most discussed ways in which they took responsibility for their siblings and how this role was re-enacted in their work.

It was interesting to note that the next largest group represented were youngest children. The therapist in this study who was the youngest sibling in her family also had the largest number of siblings (#13). She always wanted to be in a position of knowing things, in her personal life and in her work as a result of growing up as the youngest child who did not know as much as her older siblings. All of the therapist who were the youngest child from sibling groups larger than two spoke fondly of their siblings.

The impact of the youngest child position and other birth order positions were not discussed in terms of impact on sibling transference in the literature. However, in his classic work, Family Constellation, Walter Toman (1961) noted that "for the only child, even more than all other siblings, it is hard to imagine, let alone assume, any sibling position but the one he or she has actually held" (p. 114). This idea was borne out in the interview with the only child therapist in this study. She reported that, given her only child status, it may be hard for her to recognize sibling transference or give it the attention it deserves. This therapist did have difficulty responding to several questions, and although she mentioned four factors that might contribute to sibling transference, her answers were very brief and non-descriptive.

In spite of Agger's (1988) caution that self-awareness may be particularly murky regarding sibling countertransference, almost all of the respondents in this study thought of at least one aspect of their own sibling experience which might manifest in countertransference. As noted by Hamilton (1996), the subject of countertransference occupies an increasingly large place in analytic literature, and this attention in the analytic community may have contributed to the ease with which respondents spoke of it in the interviews. Sibling countertransference phenomena which they experienced included: feelings of competition, rivalry, envy, resentment, abandonment, betrayal, or caretaking with the patient; the failure to recognize sibling transference as an only child; difficulty understanding or empathizing with patients from other sibling positions; sense of romantic loss or longing with patients similar to a close or missing sibling; lower or higher

expectations of the patient's ability if they are the same gender as a sibling; the

desire for a difficult patient similar to a difficult sibling to leave treatment;

comfort with patients who are similar in some way to a sibling.

Importance of Attending to Sibling Transference

The reasons given for the importance of attending to sibling transference by

the respondents in this study are similar to those noted in the literature. This

included deepening and broadening the therapy, tapping resources in the patient

which would enhance self-development, peer and interpersonal relationships, and

the work world. The respondents failed to mention specifically release from

inhibition and anxiety regarding competition, incest, and parricide with siblings, as

postulated by Agger (1988). This may be due to those very inhibitions, but also

may be due to lack of exposure of respondents to the topic of sibling transference

in training or personal analysis.

Training

The findings of this study are consistent with the belief expressed in the

literature, namely, that there has been very little attention paid to sibling

transference in training. Again, several authors (Agger, 1988; Bank and Kahn,

1982; Lesser, 1978) stated that a personal analysis is probably the most important

aspect of training for analytic work and that inattention to sibling issues tends to

be perpetuated through this lack of attention. Given this, it seems important that training analysts and therapists become cognizant of sibling issues and transference as a means to change this cycle of neglect.

Implications for Training and Additional Implications for Practice

One approach to raise recognition of the impact of siblings on transference and treatment, in general, would be present a training module on the topic to analysts and psychotherapists in training. Given the difficulty discussed earlier in making this area more conscious and articulated for practitioners, it would be helpful to make the training personally meaningful and experiential as well as didactic. The training would be geared toward relating personal and working experiences to the literature and case examples which would facilitate the bridging between practice and theory. Because it is such an underdeveloped aspect of treatment, training approaches which aim at continuing the development of hypotheses, research, and discussion are crucial. This would contribute to the development of both grounded theory and clinical skills for practitioners.

Alexandra Kivowitz (1995) has recently argued for the kind of attention to siblings "regardless of whether siblings were left behind in the theoretical cul de sac of sibling rivalry and birth order or simply overshadowed by the mother, now that we therapists have begun to see ourselves in terms of our function as self objects and working in a complicated, intersubjective field, it may be a good time to reconsider the sibling" (p. 39).

Training would involve both information about the impact of sibling relationships in the multi-dimensional context of the family and information about how this may appear in the transference. Kivowitz (1995) again points out that early sibling relationships will need to be understood in an idiosyncratic context - integrated with, rather than separated out from other important relationships. She is referring here to past attempts that were made to compare the impact of siblings versus other family members, such as mother, father, for example, the mother has primary impact, father, second, and sibling, third. In contrast, she believes that because most sibling relationships occur in a family context, they are most often at least triangular, and quite often, even more multi-dimensional. She points out that an individual's relationship to any important person in the family context is "inter-determined" (p. 41) and refers to Solnit's (1983) statement that sibling experiences are "embedded" in the primary parent-child psychological relationship (p. 283). Kivowitz points out that no relationship of an individual child with his/her parents is ever again the same after a sibling is born, and that no relationship between siblings is, in the same sense, truly independent of the parental relational field and/or the relationship between the parent(s) or other children.

Although there is little material available on this topic, several of the articles that have been written include much rich and useful information to be included in training. To give an example, it would be helpful for a training module to cover some of the key points from Eloise Agger's (1988) excellent paper. These might include the following:

1. Clinical evidence shows that in adult life, transference aspects of a predominantly sibling nature may govern interpersonal relationships, self-concept, ego functioning, and certain phases of psychoanalytic treatment.

2. Major issues in sibling relationships that may influence ego development and identity formation are sibling rivalry, new births, sibling loss, sibling identification, and the quality of both sibling love (e.g., aim-inhibited, erotic, or incestuous) and attachment (e.g., predominantly anaclitic or narcissistic).

3. It is helpful to look for disguised reference to siblings in content that suggests incest, parricide, restitution, and atonement.

4. Frequently role diffusion, achievement aversion, and drive inhibition may be partly determined by sibling dynamics.

5. The recognition and accurate assessment of the patient's perception of siblings as significant internal objects aids in analyzing previously warded-off transference paradigms, in interpreting negative therapeutic reactions, and in reinforcing the resolution of the oedipal complex.

6. The therapist must speed up his or her reaction time in perceiving how rapidly his or her transference meaning for the patient is shifting. As Agger points out:

> At times, an hour might seem like a slide show with lights and sound effects. The slides are projected one after another in wild succession; now the therapist is seen as mother, now father, now sibling, now subject, now the whole crowd, and so forth. It's like a night back at the family dinner table. Or the aftermath of a family crisis. (p. 27)

7. Patients who were only children often form a positive attachment to the therapist based on the unconscious fantasy that he or she is their longed for

confidante and older sibling or their longed for playmate and younger sister or brother. If longings are not noted, they will endure as a resistance and block further individuation.

8. While countertransference responses within the therapist-patient mutual interaction are good indicators of sibling influence, care should be taken in formulating interpretations because the degree of one's own self-awareness may be particularly murky in this area.

Limitations of the Study

This study had several limitations. The most noticeable limitation was small sample size, only sixteen respondents. Because the sample was small, external validity is minimal. Also, internal reliability of the results may be compromised, as evidenced in some responses which had little commonality among the respondents. Therefore, interpretation of the results can only be offered tentatively.

Although an attempt was made to include some representation in age, gender, and race of the respondents, there was limited variation in all these areas, with primarily female, Caucasian respondents in their forties and early fifties agreeing to participate in the study. These three variables may be crucial in introducing bias in this study.

Bank and Kahn (1982) have proposed that therapists at mid-life (thirty-five to fifty-five) may become insensitive to difficult sibling issues of individuals in treatment if they have grown professionally active and are no longer in active conflict with their own siblings. They feel therapists in this age range may have actively repressed personal memories of conflict-laden years of childhood and adolescence. If this is the case, then the majority of the respondents in this study might have restricted their responses due to such repression.

Only three male respondents agreed to participate in this study. This definitely limited the input of male experience with siblings and transference which may differ greatly from the female experience, as discussed earlier in the interpretation of results.

Although attempts were made to include therapists from varying racial backgrounds, only two African/American therapists were able to participate, and no representative of Hispanic or Asian background. This also seems like a crucial bias for this particular study. It seems likely that race may play a significant role in how sibling relationships are structured, used, and experienced as adults. Several respondents felt that Freudian theory, with its European, Caucasian, individualistic bias significantly contributed to the lack of attention to sibling issues and transference. Given that fact, it would have been interesting to be able to include the impressions of therapists from other racial backgrounds.

Again, due to the small sample size, although some birth orders were much more represented than others there was some variation in birth order of the participants. It would have been helpful to include m ore respondents who were from other birth order variations, and greater numbers overall, particularly only children.

There was also variance in the number of years respondents had practiced and the amount of analytic training they had received. It is possible that a sample restricted to analysts who had gone through a formal analytic training program and analysis, and who had more years of experience, would have responded more easily and with greater clarity to the questions.

Another significant limitation of this study was the fact that the respondents were those who were willing to talk about this topic. This selected out therapists who were not able to discuss it, or who may feel it is unimportant, or indistinguishable from other forms of transference.

The questions covered several aspects or focus areas, and this broad coverage, in the form of 16 questions, asked in a one hour to one and one-half hour sessions, was difficult for most respondents. The length of time allotted meant that most were willing to participate and allowed for gathering information in a variety of areas. However, in some cases this contributed to gaining a small amount of information from respondents in each area, with little time to follow up or elaborate thoughts in any particular area.

One last limitation is geographic area. All of the respondents were from the San Francisco Bay Area. This meant that their views may have been influenced by a particular analytic culture of the San Francisco Area, as discussed by Victoria Hamilton (1996) in her study of the different beliefs of various analytic cultures. This may have introduced a form of cultural bias in the results.

Implications for Further Research

It would be interesting to replicate this study with a much larger sample. Recruiting a sample with greater variation in all the variables just discussed -- age, gender, race, and birth order -- might allow for the emergence and analysis of a broader array of themes and experiences. This would also allow for exploration of differences related to these variables which could not be adequately identified or explored in this study.

Adding the variable of parenting experience could add important information regarding the impact of parenting on the understanding of the impact of siblings. Two therapists in this study did state that their parenting experience helped them become aware of the feelings of a different sibling position than their own and to be more sensitive to those patients who were from different sibling positions.

Narrowing the scope of the study to gather more information in fewer topic areas might enrich understanding and gain more useful information. One respondent did ask to meet twice to complete the questions. This gave him time for the questions to resonate and enhanced his ability to respond in the second session. This was very helpful and allowed him to think more fully about his own experience and possible sibling transference in his work. Designing the study to allow for this kind of time and reflection, in a manner that would still encourage participation, would enhance the feedback.

In a study with greater representation in all the variables mentioned, sample size, race, sex, age, analytic culture, and birth order, it would be fascinating to attempt to study in more depth the interrelationship of respondent birth order and their responses to the questions.

Summary

In summary, this study examined sibling transference and countertransference in adult psychotherapy. Areas of focus included how sibling transference might manifest, particular factors contributing to the development or eliciting sibling transference, some analytic dynamics of sibling transference, respondents experience of sibling transference in theory and training, birth order and personal experiences of sibling issues relating to transference and countertransference.

All the respondents were very interested in the topic and felt that it was important. Although it was difficult for many, they were able to discuss all the focus areas to a greater or lesser degree. All respondents felt that sibling transference was neglected in their training and theory. Most were excited about greater attention to siblings in transference and countertransference and felt that this went along with newer ways of understanding the treatment relationship and transference phenomena. Attention to this does seem to be part and parcel of a movement to pay attention to the "third" area as described by Hamilton (1996). She summarizes it well in her view that analysts who subscribe to this third area "commit themselves, even if unconsciously, to pluralism, diversity, overlap, balance" (p. 3). Inclusion of siblings in our experience of transference seems to

encourage incorporation of all these attributes.

References

Agger, E. (1988). Psychoanalytic perspectives on sibling relationships. Psychoanalytic Inquiry, 8, 3-30.

Appelbaum, A. (1988). Psychoanalysis during pregnancy: The effect of sibling constellation. Psychoanalytic Inquiry, 8, 177-195.

Balint, M. (1957). The basic fault. London: Tavistock.

Bank, S. & Kahn, M. (1982). The sibling bond. New York: Basic Books.

Belenky, M. F., Clinchy, B. Mc., Goldberger, N. R., & Tarule, J. M. (1986). Women's ways of knowing. New York: Basic Books.

Bird, B. (1972). Notes on transference: Universal phenomenon and hardest part of analysis. Journal of the American Psychoanalytic Association, 20, 267-301.

Blum, H. P., & Goodman, W. H. (1995). Countertransference. In B.E. Moore & B.D. Fine (Eds.), Psychoanalysis: The major concepts. (pp. 121-129). New Haven & London: Yale University Press.

Budd, M. (1993). Wittgenstein's philosophy of psychology. London: Routledge.

Cesio, F. (1993). The Oedipal tragedy in the psychoanalytic process: Transference love. In E. S. Person, A. Hagelin, & P. Fonagy (Eds.), On Freud's "Observations on Transference-Love" (pp. 130-145). New Haven & London: Yale University Press.

Coleman, D. (1996). Positive sibling transference: Theoretical and clinical dimensions. Clinical Social Work Journal, 24, 377-387.

Erikson, E. H. (1950). Childhood and society. New York: Norton.

Fenichel, O. (1945) The psychoanalytic theory of neurosis. New York: Norton.

Freud, A. (1954). The ego and the mechanisms of defence. London: Hogarth Press. (Original work published in 1936)

Freud, S. & Breuer, J. (1955). Studies on hysteria. In J. Strachey (Ed. & Trans.), The standard edition of the complete psychological works of Sigmund Freud (vol. 2). London: Hogarth Press. (Original work published in 1895)

Freud, S. (1953). The interpretation of dreams. In J. Strachey (Ed. & Trans.), The standard Edition of the complete psychological works of Sigmund Freud (vol 4-5) London: Hogarth Press. (Original work published in 1900)

Freud, S. (1953). Three essays on the theory of sexuality. In J. Strachey (Ed. & Trans.), The standard edition of the complete psychological works of Sigmund Freud (vol. 7, pp. 125-245). London: Hogarth Press. (Original work published in 1905d)

Freud, S. (1953). Fragments of an analysis of a case of hysteria. In J. Strachey (Ed. & Trans.), The standard edition of the complete psychological works of Sigmund Freud (vol. 7, pp. 3-122). London: Hogarth Press. (Original work published in 1905e [1901])

Freud, S. (1955). Analysis of a phobia in a five-year-old boy. In J. Strachey (Ed. & Trans.), The standard edition of the complete psychological works of Sigmund Freud (vol. 10, pp. 3-149). London: Hogarth Press. (Original work published in 1909)

Freud, S. (1957). The future prospects of psycho-analysis. In J. Strachey (Ed. & Trans), The standard edition of the complete psychological works of Sigmund Freud (vol. 11, pp. 139-151). London: Hogarth Press. (Original work published in 1910)

Freud, S. (1958). The dynamics of transference. In J. Strachey (Ed. & Trans), The standard edition of the complete psychological works of Sigmund Freud (vol. 12, pp. 97-108). London: Hogarth Press. (Original work published in 1912)

Freud, S. (1955). From the history of an infantile neurosis. In J. Strachey (Ed. & Trans), The standard edition of the complete psychological works of Sigmund Freud (vol. 17, pp. 3-123). London: Hogarth Press. (Original work published in 1918 [1914])

Gill, M. (1976). The analysis of transference. Journal of the American Psychoanalytic Association, 27, 263-288.

Greenacre, P. (1966). Problems of over-idealization of the analyst and of analysis: Their manifestations in the transference and countertransference relationship. Psychoanalytic Study of the Child, 21.

Greenson, R. (1967). The technique and practice of psychoanalysis (Vol. 1). Madison: International Universities Press.

Graham, I. (1988). The sibling object and its transference: Alternative organizer of the middle field. Psychoanalytic Inquiry, 8, 88-107.

Guntrip, H. (1975). My experience of analysis with Fairbairn and Winnicott (How complete a result does psychoanalytic therapy achieve?). International Review of Psychoanalysis, 2, 145-156.

Hamilton, V. (1996). The analyst's preconscious. Hillsdale, N.J.: The Analytic Press.

Heimann, P. (1950). On counter-transference. International Journal of Psycho-Analysis, 31, 81-84.

Kaplan, L. J. (1978). Oneness and separateness. From infant to individual. New York: Simon & Schuster.

Kernberg, O. (1965). Countertransference. Journal of the American Psychoanalytic Association, 13, 38-56.

Kernberg, O. (1976). Object relations theory and clinical psychoanalysis. New York: Jason Aronson.

Kivowitz, A. (1995). Attending to sibling issues and transferences in psychodynamic psychotherapy. Clinical Social Work Journal, 23, 37-46.

Kohut, H. (1971). The analysis of the self. New York: Int. Univ. Press.

Lasky, J. F. & Mulliken, S. F. (1988). Sibling relationships and mature love. In J. F. Lasky & H. W. Silverman (Eds), Love: Psychoanalytic perspectives (pp. 81-92). New York: New York University Press.

Lesser, R. M. (1978). Sibling transference and counter-transference. Journal of the American Academy of Psychoanalysis, 6, 37-49.

Levy, S. (1984). Principles of interpretation. Northvale: Jason Aronson.

Little, M. (1951). Counter-transference and the patient's response to it. International Journal of Psycho-Analysis, 32, 32-40.

McGarty, M. (1988) The analyst's pregnancy. Contemporary Psychoanalysis, 24, 684-692.

Muir, R. (1989). Fatherhood from the perspective of object relations theory and relational systems theory. In S. Cath, A. Gurwitt, & L. Gunsberg (Eds), Fathers and their families (pp. 47-61). Hillsdale, N.J.: The Analytic Press.

Ogden, T. (1986). The matrix of the mind. Northvale: Jason Aronson.

Ogden, T. (1994). Subjects of analysis. Northvale: Jason Aronson.

Phillips, A. (1988). Winnicott. Cambridge, MA: Harvard University Press.

Provence, S. & Solnit, A. (1983). Development-promoting aspects of the sibling experience: Vicarious mastery. Psychoanalytic Study of the Child, 38, 337-351.

Rabin, H. (1989). Peers and siblings: Their neglect in analytic group psychotherapy. International Journal of Group Psychotherapy, 39, 209-221.

Racker, H. (1957). The meanings and uses of countertransference. Psychoanalytic Quarterly, 26, 303-357.

Racker, H. (1972). The meaning and uses of countertransference. Psychoanalytic Quarterly, 41, 487-506.

Reich, A. (1951). On counter-transference. International Journal of Psycho-Analysis, 32, 25-31.

Rosenbaum, M. (1963). The child raised by an older sibling. American Journal of Orthopsychiatry, 33, 515-518.

Schon, D. A. (1983). The reflective practitioner. New York: Basic Books.

Sharpe, S. A. & Rosenblatt, A. D. (1994). Oedipal sibling triangles. Journal of the American Psychoanalytic Association, 42, 491-523.

Solnit, A. (1983). The sibling experience. The Psychoanalytic Study of the Child, 38, 281-284. New Haven: Yale University Press.

Stolorow, D. & Stolorow, R. (1989). My brother's keeper: Intensive treatment of a case of delusional merger. International Journal of Psychoanalysis, 70, 315-326.

Stone, L. (1995). Transference. In B.E. Moore & B.D. Fine (Eds.), Psychoanalysis: The major concepts. (pp. 110-120). New Haven & London: Yale University Press.

Strauss, A. & Corbin, J. (1990). Basics of qualitative research. Newbury Park: Sage Publications.

Szalita, A. (1968). Reanalysis. Contemporary Psychoanalysis, 4, 83-102.

Szasz, T. (1963). The concept of transference. International Journal of Psycho-Analysis, 44, 432-443.

Toman, W. (1961). Family Constellation. New York: Spring Publishing Co.

Tower, L. (1956). Countertransference. Journal of the American Psychoanalytic Association, 4, 224-255.

Wachtel, P. (1980). Transference, schema, and assimilation: The relevance of Piaget to the psychoanalytic theory of transference. Annals of Psychoanalysis, 8, 59-76.

Winnicott, D. (1949). Hate in the counter-transference. International Journal of Psychoanalysis, 30, 69-75.

Winnicott, D. (1953). Transitional objects and transitional phenomena. In Playing and Reality. London: Tavistock, 1971.

APPENDIX A

Interview Schedule

1. I am conducting a study to better understand the occurrence of sibling transference in psychotherapy. Since you work within a psychodynamic theoretical orientation, we can assume that you also rely heavily on the transference. It might be helpful to organize your thoughts about this topic in regard to one or two cases where you have or have not worked with the sibling transference. I will be asking some specific questions about sibling transference; however I would like to begin with one that is more general. How do you define and recognize sibling transference in your practice?

2. Do you believe that sibling transference phenomena are an important aspect of treatment?

3. Do you believe that you have experienced this form of transference with your patients and if so, what thoughts, feelings, verbalizations, or actions occurred which made you feel that it may be sibling transference?

4. How do you differentiate sibling transference from parental transference?

5. How do you think a sibling transference or countertransference might be elicited or triggered in treatment?

   a. Do you feel that certain events, interpretations, or stages of therapy facilitate the development of sibling transference?

   b. If so, what might such event, interpretations, or stages be?

6. How do you think awareness of sibling transference and countertransference effect treatment?

a. What factors do you think contribute to the development of sibling transference?

b. How do you think sibling gender and therapist gender interrelate in sibling transference?

c. How do you think sibling age and therapist age interrelate?

7. What do you think the role of authority is in setting up your relationships with your patients?

a. Do you think that the authority relationships, as set up in traditional analytic therapies, might interfere with the development of sibling transference?

8. Have you experienced a sibling transference that seemed to serve as a resistance to other types of transference?

9. Conversely, have you experienced a case in which some other form of transference served as a resistance to sibling transference?

10. What is your sense of your own transference issues in regard to siblings?

a. Where are you in the birth order of your own family?

b. If you are not an only child, what age and sex are your siblings?

11. Do you think that there is a theoretical gap regarding sibling transference?

a. If you believe there is such a theoretical gap, what do you think might account for it?

12. Did you receive information regarding sibling transference or countertransference in you professional training?

13. Is there anything that I have not covered that you believe pertinent that you would like to add at this time?

APPENDIX B

Respondent's Demographics Survey

1. Gender: _____Female   _____Male

2. Age: _____

3. Birth Order: _____
                    (i.e. first born female of four, three younger brothers

4. Type of license held: _____

5. Years of licensed experience: _____

www.ingramcontent.com/pod-product-compliance
Lightning Source LLC
Chambersburg PA
CBHW070118290526

45789CB00005B/2049

* 9 781500 682255 *